COLOSSIANS

COLOSSIANS

That in all things
he might have the pre-eminence
COLOSSIANS 1:18

JOHN METCALFE

THE PUBLISHING TRUST
CHURCH ROAD, TYLERS GREEN, PENN, BUCKINGHAMSHIRE.

Printed and Published by
John Metcalfe Publishing Trust
Church Road, Tylers Green
Penn, Buckinghamshire

—

First Published 1994

—

ISBN 1 870039 55 6

—

CONTENTS

PART ONE

THE CAUSE OF PAUL'S WRITING

COLOSSIANS

THE CAUSE OF PAUL'S WRITING

AS with Ephesians, Philippians, and Philemon, the Epistle to the Colossians was written whilst Paul was in chains, a prisoner at Rome, awaiting Caesar's judgment. The distinctive feature about Colossians, however, lies in the fact that Paul had never been to the city, nor had he once preached to that people. Yet he still wrote.

There was a precedent for this in the case of the Epistle to the Romans. Years before, the apostle had written to the saints at Rome. Yet when he wrote, he had been a stranger both to the place and to the brethren. A stranger, yes; but he still wrote.

Now, albeit carried at last as a prisoner in bonds to the great Roman centre, Paul was moved to take up his pen and to write to the distant and unknown city of Colosse.

From which it is to be observed that Paul wrote to those who had never seen his face in the flesh. Why? Because in the nature of the apostolic ministry he was sent from the ascended Son of God in the glory to all saints below on earth, to the whole *ecclesia*, to the body of Christ in its entirety. 'The gospel, which ye have heard, and which was preached to every creature which is under heaven; whereof I Paul am made a minister', Col. 1:23.

From the ascended glory Paul had both seen and heard the Lord in the heavenly vision: 'Rise, and stand upon thy feet: for I have appeared unto thee for this purpose, to make thee a minister and a witness both of these things which thou hast seen, and of those things in the which I will appear unto thee; delivering thee from the people, and from the Gentiles, unto whom now I send thee', Acts 26:16,17: then, to all the Gentiles, the whole world. 'A debtor both to the Greeks, and to the Barbarians', Rom. 1:14; hence, 'Necessity is laid upon me; yea, woe is unto me, if I preach not the gospel!' I Cor. 9:16.

Nor is preaching the gospel to every creature all: indissolubly joined with it was the teaching which that gospel includes: 'to make all see what is the fellowship of the mystery', Eph. 3:9; 'according to my gospel, and the preaching of Jesus Christ, according to the revelation of the mystery', Rom. 16:25. 'For I have not shunned to declare unto you all the counsel of God', Acts 20:27. Thus, 'I now rejoice in my sufferings for you, and fill up that which is behind of the afflictions of Christ in my flesh for his body's sake, which is the church: whereof I am made a minister', Col. 1:24,25.

Paul's ministry began in preaching where Christ was not named, that is, in the regions beyond, throughout the whole world, 'the minister of Jesus Christ to the Gentiles', Rom. 15:16. But that ministry proceeded further, as it ought, from the beginning of the gospel to its effectual end: 'the perfecting of the saints, the work of the ministry, the edifying of the body of Christ: till we all come in the unity of the faith, and of the knowledge of the Son of God, unto a perfect man, unto the measure of the stature of the fulness of Christ', Eph. 4:12,13.

That is it: to all saints; to the whole body. Whether in person or by epistle. Therefore, though a stranger, he writes to the Colossians, and, besides them, even to 'as many as have not seen my face in the flesh', Col. 2:1. A minister to all saints; the entire *ecclesia*; the whole body.

The occasion of writing to the saints at Colosse presented itself with the visit of Epaphras to the apostle Paul at Rome. Epaphras was a minister and faithful servant to the brethren at Colosse and in the parts round about. He preached the grace of God in truth with great fervour in the congregations at Hierapolis, Laodicea, and Colosse. Withal he laboured and strove incessantly in fervent prayer for them, their welfare being deeply engraved on his heart.

This Epaphras, seeking out the apostle Paul at Rome, had learned from him the full revelation of the grace of God in the gospel, a light above all that he had received hitherto. This communication kindled his zeal, making him the more anxious that the saints to whom he ministered should receive the same benefit, to the praise of the glory of God's grace: 'That their hearts might be comforted, being knit together in love, and unto all riches of the full assurance of understanding, to the acknowledgement of the mystery of God, and of the Father, and of Christ', Col. 2:2. He, with the apostle, strove for them in prayer to this end.

But the apostle, a prisoner in chains, could not travel with him to fulfil this ministry according to the earnest desire of

3

Epaphras, who the more diligently conveyed to Paul every concern and the clearest testimony in respect of the saints assembled at Colosse.

The consequence of such interior heart labour and supplication, and such intense love, with all carefulness, between the two fellowlabourers, brought to pass the writing of the Epistle to the Colossians. Thus the apostle Paul, entreated by Epaphras, sought to accomplish by letter, so far as it was possible, what he could not fulfil by bodily presence.

From which it follows, as to the cause of Paul's writing, that the first reason for the epistle was to make known to the saints and faithful brethren at Colosse the glorious revelation of the Son of God in the gospel committed to Paul. Here note that although Epaphras was enlightened as a faithful minister of the word, he saw in this no reason to be high-minded, but the rather this fact caused him humbly to press Paul that he might be instructed more perfectly in the heavenly light of the gospel of Christ. And not only so, but he showed an equal zeal that the apostle should minister to his brethren at Colosse, that they might receive the like benefit also.

Whence observe that, however zealous, we ought correspondingly to be of a lowly and humble mind—even if, especially if—ministers of the word, so as meekly to receive those holy apostles, and chosen vessels, sent down from the Head to bring the whole body into the unity of the faith, and of the knowledge of the Son of God, unto a perfect man, unto the measure of the stature of the fulness of Christ.

Likewise that all might answer to the fellowship of the mystery, the body of Christ, to the intent that now unto the principalities and powers in the heavenly places might be made known by the *ecclesia* the manifold wisdom of God, according to the eternal purpose which he hath purposed in Christ Jesus our Lord.

The corollary of this is to be seen in the earnest zeal of the saints to grow up in Christ, to grow in grace and in the knowledge of the truth, and, if so, to receive the ministry sent for this very purpose. Evidently, in the new testament, the brethren were fervent in the Spirit, panting after the knowledge of the Son of God, not only individually, but together, growing up in one body unto the Head in all things.

That is, the brethren were united in worship not only in their own assembly in any given locality, but in the whole assembly on earth uniting every locality. They were thus conscious of one Spirit, one body, one hope of their calling; one Lord, one faith, one baptism; one God and Father of all, who is above all, and through all and in all.

It was God's assembly; his dwelling; he indwelt all the saints in every assembly, so constituting the one assembly—'my *ecclesia*: my assembly'—the house of God, which is the assembly of the living God, the pillar and ground of the truth.

This brought in and maintained the consciousness of what the saints were as one body to Christ, one house for God, and one temple of the Holy Ghost. This elevated the minds of the saints to the true nature of the *ecclesia*: that it is God's, a thing far exceeding all that is personal, and everything merely local or earthly. It is to this that the saints were called, and are called, and which they were to receive with joy, from the ministry sent down from above.

This is amply demonstrated in the Epistle to the Colossians. The saints at Colosse had embraced Christ whole-heartedly to the full measure of Epaphras' ministry. Nevertheless, both he and they, hearing of the dispensation of the grace of God committed to Paul, earnestly sought the benefit of this revelation of the mystery of Christ. In all humility and lowliness of mind, commonly aware of the relative limitation of the gift, calling, and spiritual knowledge of Epaphras' service—and none more so than Epaphras himself—with one accord the saints sent unto Paul at Rome.

The meekness of Epaphras is demonstrated in his being foremost to acknowledge the need of the apostolic ministry. And now, at Rome, Epaphras' entreaty of Paul on his own and on their behalf stood in their common earnest desire for the light of the glory to break forth upon them in the fulness of the blessing of the gospel of Christ by the service of this chosen vessel, Paul, the apostle sent to the Gentiles.

Here is seen, therefore, a cause for the writing of the Epistle to the Colossians: to make known to the saints at Colosse, further to their then understanding and experience of the gospel of Christ, the full revelation of the knowledge of the Son of God, manifest in the hope of the gospel, as it had been entrusted to Paul for this purpose.

He could not come, but he did write: 'The prisoner of Jesus Christ for you Gentiles, if ye have heard of the dispensation of the grace of God which is given me to you-ward: how that by revelation he made known unto me the mystery; as I wrote afore in few words, whereby, when ye read, ye may understand my knowledge in the mystery of Christ.' This to the Ephesians, Eph. 3:1-4.

But it is equally true of the Colossians: 'Even the mystery which hath been hid from ages and from generations, but now is made manifest to his saints: to whom God would make known what is the riches of the glory of this mystery among the Gentiles; which is Christ in you, the hope of glory: whom we preach, warning every man, and teaching every man in all wisdom; that we may present every man perfect in Christ Jesus: whereunto I also labour, striving according to his working, which worketh in me mightily', Col. 1:26-29.

When new-born babes the Colossians had desired the sincere milk of the word, which Epaphras, according to the grace given unto him, had been able to minister in abundance. Now, however, growing in grace and coming into spiritual maturity, the saints yearned after the strong meat, that they might become skilful in the word of righteousness, with one accord holding fast the Head in all wisdom and spiritual understanding. For this they hungred.

And it was precisely this appetite that the apostle Paul, through his unique ministry, was equipped to satisfy, that they might be nourished and increased, as is so evident from the doctrine and substance of the Epistle to the Colossians.

Furthermore there is an urgency in Paul's epistle concerning the growth of the Colossians. This is because of the frailty of babes, the vulnerability of the immature, the exposure of the ignorant, and the instability of the novice. This can be met by nothing other than the knowledge of the truth:

'As he spake these words, many believed on him. Then said Jesus to those Jews which believed on him, If ye continue in my word, then are ye my disciples indeed; and ye shall know the truth, and the truth shall make you free', Jn. 8:30-32. 'They are not of the world, even as I am not of the world. Sanctify them through thy truth:thy word is truth',Jn.17:16,17.

'God hath from the beginning chosen you to salvation through sanctification of the Spirit and belief of the truth: whereunto he called you by our gospel, to the obtaining of the glory of our Lord Jesus Christ', II Th. 2:13,14. 'But grow in grace, and in the knowledge of our Lord and Saviour Jesus Christ. To him be glory both now and for ever. Amen', II Peter 3:18.

'For this cause we also, since the day we heard it, do not cease to pray for you, and to desire that ye might be filled with the knowledge of his will in all wisdom and spiritual understanding', Col. 1:9.

In connection with this fervent desire of the apostle for the saints at Colosse, there is a secondary—but hardly less urgent —consideration. This permeates the Epistle to the Colossians: Namely, their need for growth in grace and in the knowledge of the truth was accelerated by the great dangers posed by so many subtle deceivers everywhere abroad in religion. Hence another cause for the epistle is discovered in the apostle's concern lest they be turned aside by false teachers full of cunning craftiness and plausible philosophies.

Thus it was essential in the apostolic ministry to warn the assemblies of every error, and of all forms of heresy. More: to alert the saints to the high authority of spiritual wickedness in heavenly places, the vast range of the powers of darkness, the swarming hordes of deceitful men—and of sincere men being deceived—who, if they could, would beguile the babes in Christ, bewitch the immature, and lead the naïve and ignorant out of the way of righteousness.

Already—after so short a time—the world was full of deceitful errors against the truth, of debasing corruptions contrary to the word of God, of perversions defiling the gospel, and of travesties parodying the nature of the new testament, all appealing to the carnal mind, flattering to the will of man, and suited to the gratification of the flesh in religion. Received, these could only lead to destruction.

It was therefore the profound concern of the apostle that the saints should not only be warned of the prevalent forms of error, but, whilst being built up and fortified in the faith, that they should ever be alert as one body to recognise, repudiate, and resist the numerous variations of false teaching, erroneous doctrine, specious heresies, and increasing corruptions that would yet arise, and abound, not diminish, so much the more as the day approached.

The pestilential busybodies propagating the errors then present, and much more those yet to come, would incessantly and insidiously seek introduction into the hearts and minds of individual brethren, of the families of the saints, and of groups of the faithful whom circumstances or preference had brought together, thence to penetrate into the very *ecclesia* itself. By such a strategy, using diverse tactics, the powers of darkness governed by the Adversary would seek the division of the *ecclesia*, the apostasy of the saints, the corruption of the gospel, and the ruin of the testimony, from generation to generation, and from age to age, without cessation or intermission, till the end of time.

Against this, striving mightily in prayer, and labouring constantly in the truth, the apostle fought on behalf of the saints with every spiritual weapon, both for the time then present, and with a view to the future, laying down principles for those yet to be called, even until the last day, when the Lord should descend from the glory to gather together his elect from the four winds, from one end of heaven to the other.

Hence it is to be observed that in Colossians the apostle both warns and straitly admonishes the brethren of those errors prevalent at the time, and in the place, to which by nature they were the most exposed. He speaks particularly against any sophism—the speculation of the natural mind in morals and religion—and of artful juggling—corruptions of the old testament lawlessly reintroduced.

In turn, Paul warns of philosophy; of vain deceit after the traditions of men; of the rudiments of this world; of the old testament shadows concerning meat, drink, holy days, new moons, and sabbaths; of voluntary humility; of worshipping of angels; of intruding into things unseen; of being puffed up in the fleshly mind; of being subject to ordinances, command-ments, and doctrines of men; and, finally, of making a show of wisdom in will worship, voluntary humility, bodily neglect, and deliberately dishonouring the flesh in a way of human invention neither required, desired, or commanded of God.

It may well have been that the apostle's warnings and admonitions to the Colossians were more than rhetorical: that the corruption was not only at the doors, but had gained some entrance. It is certain that the hordes of false prophets, deceitful workers, legalistic teachers, and self-sent ministers, who plagued the early church, had swarmed as far as Colosse. These wretched opportunists even at that very time attempted to beguile the simple, bewitch the naïve, and besmirch the pure.

They came with enticing words of man's wisdom, with great swelling assertions of authority, in a manner suited to the flesh, and conforming to this world. Such false teachers, claiming earthly ordination (particularly from Jerusalem) used the old testament—then the entire bible—with great guile and much skilfulness, as they had at Corinth; Galatia; with the Hebrews; and were yet to do, as it would appear in due course from the epistles of John.

It was deceitful workers of this sort who trailed after Paul—at a safe distance—throughout his fruitful ministry. No sooner had the apostle departed to labour for Christ in regions beyond, than these insinuated themselves into the congregations he had just left. Immediately they set about to deride his doctrine and slander his person. He was represented as a fanatical individualist without proper authority—that is, from Jerusalem—isolated, and quite unable to work with others.

These having neither revelation, call, nor fruit of their own, took the liberty of plundering the fruitfulness of the man they derided in his absence, taking advantage of the work of God so manifest in the ministry of Christ's servant, without shame or scruple, not hesitating to revile his saving doctrine or his sent ministry.

The canker of these false apostles, however, had not spread at Colosse to the degree that it had in Galatia. This may be because they were aware that Paul, in chains at Rome, had not visited Colosse. No doubt, however, storm enough would be raised when these evil workers heard of the Epistle to the Colossians, which, like all Paul's epistles, weighty and powerful, were the death knell of these evil workers and of their corrupt perversions of the faith.

Certainly Paul kept in remembrance his experience of the Galatians. In that place the saints had in fact embraced the perversions of the gospel, and slanders against the apostle in his person and ministry, put out by these false ministers. Having gained that ground, next, by their craft and subtlety, these pestilential sectaries beguiled the brethren, leading them under the law, ensnaring them in works, so as finally to entangle them again in the yoke of bondage.

Having left Galatia, Paul afterwards heard what took place in his absence. He writes to them in an epistle, expostulating against their infidelity, marvelling that they had so soon removed from him that called them into the grace of Christ unto another gospel. Thus the apostle enforced the truth that there was no other gospel than that which he had preached to them by the revelation of Jesus Christ at the beginning.

There was salvation by no other doctrine. Law and grace were incompatible. Faith and works were diametrically opposed. This world and the next could not be reconciled. It must be all of one, or all of the other. So Paul vehemently pressed home the danger in which the Galatians stood.

In Colosse, however, such a state—though a possibility—had not yet developed. Rather, what appeared at Colosse was an inordinate enchantment with the forms of the old covenant, the law ordained by angels, the being and activity of heavenly authorities, all viewed through the glass of loose philosophical speculation.

This was well adapted to the carnal mind, and the natural energy of the flesh, in that religion which man supposes to be agreeable with what he thinks of as God. This blasphemy is what the Epistle to the Colossians demolishes with such devastating effect by the revelation of the glory of Christ through the pen of the apostle Paul.

PART TWO
THE ESSENCE OF THE DOCTRINE

PART TWO

THE ESSENCE OF THE DOCTRINE

THE essence of the apostle's doctrine? In Colossians? What, with their 'worshipping of angels', Col. 2:18? With 'things invisible', Col. 1:16? 'Created in heaven'? With their 'intruding into those things which they had not seen', Col. 2:18? With 'thrones, dominions, principalities, and powers', invisible, and in the heavenlies, Col. 1:16? With 'voluntary humility', that God neither commanded nor sought, Col. 2:18? What is all this, and what essential doctrine is called forth from the apostle in relation to it?

Modern education and Western materialism has so dulled the senses of the people—and so infiltrated the professing church—that there is no longer any awareness of a world other than that of the visible and tangible: no consciousness of a world spiritual and supernatural, beyond the senses. Again, the sheer weight of worldliness and earthiness, backed by the illusion of the invincibility of science—falsely so-called— has resulted in modern man supposing that there are no beings other or higher than himself.

Primitive peoples had more sense. At least they were cogniz-
ant of demons, or of spirits, and, feeling that these must be
placated, revolved their lives around superstitions and fears
brought about by this awareness being exaggerated beyond
reason. Nevertheless, at least they knew that spirits existed,
they were acutely conscious of the being of demons, they were
fully aware of another world, a supernatural world, just beyond
the visible.

Of this, but in a more enlightened way, the Colossians were
also conscious. More enlightened, because they knew that
this other world was not merely populated by demons and
malicious spirits, but likewise by angels, principalities, powers,
and dominions. To these, however, they paid servile homage,
and, in gross superstition (though not so blind as that of the
primitive heathen) worshipped the angels.

To the churches and denominations of today, this is ridicu-
lous. To them, in practice, there are neither angels, spirits,
nor demons. As to principalities and powers, they know not
whether there be any principalities or powers. All this is as
illogical to them now, as it was to the Sadducees then. To
present-day Christendom these things do not exist, and hence
it follows that they cannot exist. Then, Colossians is a mean-
ingless book. Its essential doctrine is pointless. It is irrelevant.
Its very essence has no basis in fact. And facts, visible, tangible,
pragmatic facts, are all that matters to the modern world and
its so-called churches.

Quite the opposite, Colossians was written to a people acutely
aware of the supernatural, of another dimension beyond time
and sense, of the existence not only of a spirit world, but of
one populated by both good and bad invisible powers of vast
numbers and of complex governmental structure. High in this
structure were the angels. Sensing this (beyond all worldly
phenomena and material facts) and sensing the superiority
of such a world to all that was merely visible, temporal, or

transient, the Colossians were intensely aware of a spiritual universe now quite beyond the conception of debased modern man.

More: the Colossians knew of the activity of the angels throughout the old testament, and particularly in the giving of the law, 'Ordained by angels in the hands of a mediator', Gal. 3:19. They therefore worshipped these supernatural beings of such vast power and age-long existence, placed in positions of great authority and significance in relation to all that subsisted below.

But the Colossians were called saints. They ought not to bow to the creature. It is true that they knew far more than their contemporaries, who, 'professing themselves to be wise, became fools', Rom. 1:22. Just as their knowledge greatly exceeded that of this present day and age, a motley accumulation produced through the machinery of conveyor belt education, run on the weak fuel—liberally vitiated—of materialistic science. But for all that, the Colossians were not wise.

Though having been apprehended by the grace of Christ, though believing the truth of the gospel, nevertheless they had little understanding—and it would appear even less interest— in the relationship of the Son of God to that supernatural realm of which they made so much but knew so little. Puffed up, they would meddle and presume in things which they had never seen.

However that wherein they lacked vision had been revealed to faith in the gospel: Christ was head over all principality and power; in the revelation of the mystery he was Head of the body; it pleased the Father that in him should all fulness dwell; and the end was this: that in all things he should have the pre-eminence.

As to the invisible principalities, powers, thrones, and dominions, the whole sphere of invisible government in the heavenlies, the Colossians ought to be more circumspect.

First, the Son of God created all. Second, he was above all. Third, he would terminate all. And, Fourth, he himself would create a new order in that same supernatural realm of which, from first to last, he was the head, the Alpha and the Omega, the beginning and the ending.

Head over all, head of all principality and power, and—in a mystery exceeding all—Head of the body. This was that body of which they themselves were members, in union with the Head. This was the mystery of Christ, and, below it, their vision should never have been allowed to decline. And if not their vision, how much less their homage? What then were they doing?

It is precisely this that Colossians sets in so strong a light, showing the position of Christ in relation to that supernatural order, and the relation of that invisible and heavenly authority to him. This is to elevate the worship of the saints, according to the truth of the gospel, to him who is over all; and in him, and through him, and by him, to God and the Father of our Lord Jesus Christ.

The Epistle to the Colossians declares the saints' deliverance in Christ out of the entire realm of this present world; beyond the heavens and earth now existent; out of the old man; from the body of this flesh; clear of the whole authority of darkness. The elect are seen as having been translated into an absolutely new realm, the kingdom of God's dear Son, the inheritance of the saints in light, soon to be made manifest at the appearing and revelation of Jesus Christ.

This was what Christ had effected, and what he will put into effect. The relationship of his person to the old, the first, creation appears. The relation of his work to the old, the first, creation is made manifest. The relationship which Christ bears to the elect is revealed: it is one in which he has accomplished the reality of their circumcision, the spirituality of their baptism, and both in the body of his flesh through death. This, before they were so much as called. It was this redemption that took them out of the entire old realm, in and by himself alone, and all from the Father, or ever they came to faith.

The sheer immensity of the Son of God and his doctrine radiates throughout the epistle. This reveals the body of Christ in a standing and experience of grace truly breath-taking in the vastness of its scope. It is the Son's exaltation over all the heavens and the earth in new, risen, glorified manhood that achieved this.

In the days of his flesh no more than a little lower than the angels, now he is head over all, far above all, and at that in the very same manhood which the Son had taken to himself, and in which he went below all and under all, in his humiliation.

He was in the form of God; he thought it not robbery to be equal with God; but he made himself of no reputation; he took upon him the form of a servant—made a little lower than the angels for the suffering of death—and was made in the likeness of men: and being found in fashion as a man, he humbled himself, and became obedient unto death, even the death of the cross. By himself he purged our sins. He descended into the lower parts of the earth, or ever he rose to the heights of the glory.

Wherefore God hath highly exalted him, and given him a name which is above every name: that at the name of Jesus every knee should bow, of things in heaven, and things in earth, and things under the earth. Crowned with glory and honour, exalted to the right hand of the Majesty on high, seated on the throne of his Father, all authority has been given unto him who reigns above all things created, visible and invisible, in this world, and in that which is to come: to whom be glory and dominion for ever and ever. Amen.

Christ has ascended far over all, that he might fill all things. For now he hath obtained—in risen and exalted manhood—a more excellent name than that of angels. Now it is 'Let all the angels of God worship him'; for unto the angels hath God not put in subjection the world to come: no, it is the inheritance of sonship, of the Son in glorified manhood, together with that body chosen in him before the foundation of the world.

The exaltation of the second man, the last Adam, the quickening spirit, to the throne of glory, through an ascension far above all principalities, powers, lordships, dominions, beyond all angels, over every name that is named, not only in this world, but that which is to come, that exaltation, I say, did it: it effected everything, giving place and honour to the Son in glorified and new manhood, the first begotten from the dead, to change everything according to the will of God and his Father. This is called 'reconciliation'. And it is of the essence in Colossians.

This took the saints, the elect of God, from under the authority of darkness; out of the debtor's prison; beyond death; clear of the old enmity; past the ancient alienation; free from the body of sin; beyond this present age; above the apostasy; over the rudiments of this world; released from the handwriting of ordinances which was against them and contrary to them; discharged from the principalities and powers in the heavenlies; redeemed from sins and trespasses; loosed from the bondage of corruption; and delivered from the wrath and judgment to come.

This brought those once dead in sin into being numbered with the saints; being called Faithful brethren; being found in Christ; having God as their Father; being under the word of the truth of the gospel; having received the grace of God in truth; being made partakers of the inheritance of the saints in light; into the hope which was laid up for them in heaven; into sonship; into reconciliation; into the body of Christ; into the *ecclesia*; into the kingdom of God's dear Son; into union with Christ; into the riches of the glory of this mystery among the Gentiles, which was Christ in them, the hope of glory.

This brought them into peace; being under the inestimable benefits of the apostolic ministry; being complete in Christ; being heirs of the world to come; being members of the new, heavenly, man; being risen with Christ; being circumcised and baptized through the death, burial, and resurrection of Christ; being quickened together with Christ; being rooted and built up in Christ; being stablished in Christ; having their inward life hidden with Christ in God; and having the certain hope of appearing with Christ in glory.

This brought them into being called the elect of God, holy and beloved; being inwardly ruled by the peace of God; being richly indwelt by the word of Christ in all wisdom; being full of grace in their hearts, singing to the Lord in psalms, hymns, and spiritual songs; doing everything in the name of the Lord Jesus, giving thanks to God and the Father by him; and it brought them under the apostolic blessing and benediction, namely, 'Grace be with you. Amen.'

The essence of this epistle appears in sharp contrast with the unhallowed philosophizing and carnal speculation of the Colossians regarding this present Creation comprising the entire age from the first day to the last, from the foundation of the world to its dissolution, from the beginning of time to the end of it.

Doubtless during the vast period, under the old testament, God both spoke and wrought, especially as it pertains to the giving of the law. But he did this through angels. Just as the government of the heavens and earth had been committed from the beginning to the varied offices and authorities of angelic principalities and powers.

But whatever God did, or had done, and whatever govern-mental order he had established, all was in relation to this Creation, and this present world. And however God had spoken, or whatever he had given in a way of law or ordinances, statutes or commandments, precepts or judgments, all was for man alive in this present world, no more, and all was ordained by angels.

With the coming of Christ, and the work of Christ, and the exaltation of Christ, everything changed. All the old was judged. Judgment had been passed on this present world, 'Of judgment, because the prince of this world is judged', Jn. 16:11, 'Now is the judgment of this world: now shall the prince of this world be cast out', Jn. 12:31. All this present creation is now past in the judgment of God, the counsels of God, the will of God, and the purpose of God.

All of the old, but every part of it, God now calls 'The rudiments of this world'. In Christ the saints, all saints, the whole body, the entire *ecclesia*, all who should ever be called, were dead to it. They looked for another. They looked for another world, a world to come; they looked for an eternity past this present age; for a new creation after the first had passed away; they looked for a new, heavenly man; for a new heavens and a new earth the spiritual government of which had been reconciled by Christ and unto him. The saints were utterly dead to the first, and wholly alive to the second.

The vision of Christ in Colossians is one in which his work in heaven and earth has been completed, and completed through death. Now he is ascended into heaven. He is exalted to the glory. But in manhood. New, heavenly, manhood. This appears in the expression at the outset, 'God and the Father of our Lord Jesus Christ', Col. 1:3, where the title 'Lord Jesus Christ' declares his ascended glory. However, since the same place refers to his 'God', evidently it points to him in that ascended glory as Man, risen man, in that very manhood which he, who ever was the divine Son, had taken to himself in indissoluble union at the incarnation. That, he took down into death.

Now, risen in that same manhood from the dead, ascended and seated in the glory, he assumes the place of Head of a new order of sonship to be created after his own heavenly image. The old man is dead. But a new, heavenly man reigns in glory, head over all, the man beloved of God, the man of whom it is said 'The God and Father of our Lord Jesus Christ'.

In deity he created all things. In manhood he inherits all things. And for the coming day of this inheritance, together with every heir of promise, the entire body of Christ, he waits in hope, seated on his Father's throne in heavenly glory.

The position of the saints in Colossians is seen as one of having died with Christ to all below: the old man; the old creation; the old age; the legal realm; the sphere of this world; the old heavens and earth; the old governmental order; the entire rudiments of this world. The saints are dead to it all, having died with Christ, and having been buried with him out of sight from off the face of the earth. Now, they are risen with him. That is their standing in Christ.

The Colossian position is not that of being seated together in heavenly places in Christ, as in Ephesians. It is not that of being pilgrims through the wilderness of this present world, journeying to the heavenly country, as in Hebrews. It is not that of being the temple of the Holy Ghost on earth in the midst of this present evil age, as in Corinthians. It is not that of being quickened into the awareness of death and burial with Christ, as in Romans.

It is that of being risen with Christ from the dead, whilst still on earth, with Christ viewed on high at the right hand of God and the Father, reigning above all heavens. In a mystery, the saints below are filled with the life of the Son from above. Whilst they are on earth, and he in glory, still, Christ is in them the hope of glory. From the Head on high, risen life fills the body below. He is their life; that is, inwardly, who was

23

raised, and is ascended, for whose coming from heaven they wait on earth with patience.

It is of the essence to grasp the truth that Christ is in heaven in terms, first, of Manhood, and second, of an entirely new order of Manhood. This Manhood is that of the Son, and, in him and from him, that of sonship. This Manhood is already—even now—exalted in heaven, and is at once spiritual, heavenly, mysterious, divine, glorious, and everlasting, having its existence on the other side of death, from the glory, in a word, from God out of heaven. This Manhood is not for this world, it is for the world to come.

The elect, chosen of the Father, holy and beloved, are seen as united to Christ in one body, filled with the Spirit of sonship and destined for the inheritance of the saints in light. The saints are not reconciled with a view to this world, but in view of the world to come. They wait for the world to come: it is their hope. Waiting for his appearing. Waiting for the resurrection. Waiting for the inheritance. And, whilst waiting, dead to all that is of the earth beneath and to the constitution and age that now exist. That is of the essence in Colossians.

The life of the Son on high fills the body below. It is not that the Spirit is referred to here: it is the life of Christ that fills the body below. The Spirit is not mentioned in Colossians, save possibly on one occasion. It is Christ himself who must be apprehended, and that in the full knowledge of his person and work. The Spirit does not speak of himself in Colossians: he takes the things of Christ and shows them to the saints. Moreover, he shows them things to come.

I say, it is the life of Christ himself that fills the body, so constituting one new man. But it is the Head who is glorified, and glorified in behalf of the body. The glory of the Head is wonderfully exalted, and manifested to all the body below, through the meek and lowly service of him who speaks not of himself, but, receiving of the things of Christ, shows them unto the saints, so as to glorify the Head by revealing the greatness—the sheer vastness—of his person and work: that is Colossians. Essentially it is Colossians.

Christ is in glory. Yes, but he is in glory as Head over the body, yet one with that body. That is the mystery. Again and again the word Mystery occurs. But it is a mystery revealed, one into which we enter experimentally, one which is to be realized, a mystery that is now made known to his saints. Not that we fathom it: but in experiencing it, we know it: 'That God would make known unto you the fellowship of the mystery.'

This mystery 'hath been hid from ages and from generations, but now is made manifest to his saints: to whom God would make known what is the riches of the glory of this mystery among the Gentiles; which is Christ in you, the hope of glory', Col. 1:26,27. That is it: a mystery made known. Of this mystery divided Christendom is oblivious, and from it evangelicalism has apostatized. Nevertheless to its rediscovery and realization we are called anew in these last days by the gospel.

We are dead on earth. We have died with Christ. Then, likewise, we are risen with him on earth. The risen life from the Head in heaven fills us in a mystery here below, united —visibly united: really one—in a new, another, a glorious heavenly man. One new man. And this in the midst of the scene of Christ's rejection. Our Head, who is our life, was, and still is, rejected here below. The old man would have none of him, and it will have none of us in whom he dwells.

This world is an alien world, with an alien philosophy, a world whose religion perverts a past covenant in the darkness. This world, this age, this passing time is nothing short of a sphere of alienation from God, with nothing but enemies of God around, above, below, and about.

Although Christ created offices and governments in heaven above and the earth below, visible and invisible, yet all has become alienated in the Fall. Nothing but alienation exists below, and exists below in total moral darkness, blinded and deceived by the god of this world. Here, only one thing is of God: it is the one body of Christ, visibly united according to divine purpose. But practically denied according to man's apostasy.

It is to the recovery of this that we are now called by the gospel in one body. For, 'We know that we are of God, and the whole world lieth in wickedness', I Jn. 5:19.

The existing age, and this present world, despite the law given in it by the mediation of angels as a rule of righteousness for earthly Israel—which was never kept: 'Who have received the law by the disposition of angels, and have not kept it'—all, but all, is nothing other than a realm of unbroken darkness and death.

This present age is the realm of the Fall, of fallen earthy Adam, of the man of sin and death, of the god of this world, of the spiritual rulers of the darkness of this world. Nothing of God is left on earth but the *ecclesia*, the body of Christ, the house of God, the pillar and ground of the truth: and this is to be one: visibly one, one in any given place, and one in every place.

It is precisely this which disobedient evangelicalism, having apostatized in wilful ignorance, refuses even to admit as a reality: but it is also precisely this for which Christ died and on which his heart is set that it should be recovered. But such a recovery must of necessity appear in a realm where all around is darkness, stretching back to the beginning of time and reaching forward till time shall be no more.

This darkness is a moral state which must and shall prevail in heaven above and in the earth beneath until the last day, when Christ, having come for his own out of the world, will turn out the old incumbents, dissolve the present heavens and earth, and bring in a new heavens and new earth wherein dwelleth righteousness. This coming creation is called the everlasting inheritance, with every office, order, and government reconciled according to the purpose of him who worketh all things after the counsel of his own will.

This is the essence of the doctrine of Paul the apostle to the saints and faithful brethren in Christ at Colosse. There follows the argument of the epistle, the opening of which reveals the apostle's doctrine—interwoven with prayer, exhortation, and experimental application—presented in due order, unfolding sequence, and proper balance for the comfort, admonition, and edification of the brethren at Colosse.

PART THREE

THE ARGUMENT OF THE EPISTLE

THE ARGUMENT OF THE EPISTLE

COLOSSIANS exemplifies a fact more or less manifest in all the epistles: that it is impossible to reduce these letters to a system of precise, analytical deduction. Intellectual study simply will not suffice in order to discover the flow of the argument in these divine communications.

Paul neither wrote from cold logic, nor was it his intention to develop some academic proposition. His letters were not marketable correspondence courses, neither was he a lecturer to some classroom of students whose function it was to receive religious education.

Paul wrote out of the burning issues of eternity ablaze in his own heart, kindled in the light of the revelation from the Father in heaven, conceived in union with Christ in the glory, and issuing forth through the power and inworking of the Holy Ghost below.

The inner man of the apostle was alight with divine illumination: his passions, his affections, his bowels of mercies moved to the depths for the love and care which he bore to all the saints, and—in the case of this letter—to the saints at Colosse in particular.

Throughout the Epistle to the Colossians revelation flows into thanksgiving; thanksgiving into prayer; prayer into desire for the growth of the saints; the growth of the saints into their need for doctrine; their need for doctrine into admonition against deceivers; admonition against deceivers into warnings of false teaching; warnings of false teaching into exhortation to walk in the heavenly ministry of Christ.

All springs from Paul's heart, everything flows through his affections, the whole shines in his mind, being drawn forth by his ardent love for the elect, holy and beloved.

Detached intellect, cloistered study, notional education, will never reach to these things. Only the like living experience, the like call to the ministry, the like inward frames, the like divine revelation, the like decades of discipline, will discover the secret.

Those out of the secret, the whole carnal brood, may therefore do us the kindness of throwing away the dead and dry old commentaries which they have exhumed, together with the pen and paper with which they plagiarize them, and, as a necessary charity to us all, kindly lay down the charges and actually blow up all their faculties, schools, seminaries, colleges, classrooms, desks and all into the bargain.

Opening the epistle, the apostle is obviously concerned to declare the hope of the gospel, Col. 1:1 to 2:5.

He commences with the apostolic benediction, first by stating his divine authority, then associating brother Timothy with him in the apostolate by the will of God.

All was of grace. If so, according to the election of God in Christ Jesus from eternity, the justification of the chosen in Christ Jesus by substitutionary atonement in time, and the effectual inworking of faith by the Holy Ghost in due season.

Otherwise grace were no more grace. But grace is grace. The elect had done nothing, and could do nothing. God had done everything.

This was called Grace, and such grace could bring nothing but peace. Grace brought to light the election of God and the Father; grace brought in sonship; grace was wholly of God; grace was nothing of man.

Grace was of heaven not earth; of Christ not Adam; of the Spirit not the flesh; of the world to come not the world that now is; grace was of the new Creation not the old. In a word, in the new testament, everything, but everything, was of grace.

Of grace, yes, but expressed in sonship, an entirely new, heavenly, divine, glorious revelation: the revelation of the mystery. This was from God 'our Father', and, if so, not of flesh and blood, but entirely distinct from it. Distinct from the old man, the first birth, the world, the age, and all that is in and of the earth.

Through the distinctive work of God 'our Father' the saints were called Sons. This was because of the generation of the Father in heaven, through the revelation of the Son within their hearts upon earth.

Begotten of God, the saints were called out of the world, and into grace and peace. Every utterance of this call, every standing of this grace, every experience of this breathing, and every generation of God and the Father, being in and through the Lord Jesus Christ.

This calling was through the apostolic ministry. Neither—though the apostles have ceased—has this ministry ceased, though it must be subject. Hence, if the Lord but favour our generation, 'brother Timotheus' becomes a reality in our own times, just as the words indicated a principle when Paul wrote.

This answers the four questions of Romans 10:14,15, each ultimately addressing the criterion of the authority of Christ in the gospel: 'How then shall they call on him in whom they have not believed? And how shall they believe in him of whom they have not heard? And how shall they hear without a preacher? And how shall they preach except they be sent?'

The pretensions of popery, the collapse of Anglicanism, and the jettisoning of authority by independency, do nothing at all to address these agonising, vital questions, of all the most central. Nevertheless both the foundation and the seal of God stand sure. 'I am the LORD; I change not.'

Then neither can immutable new testament principles nor unalterable divine ways change. The more especially as it pertains to authority and the communication of salvation from the ministry of the Lord Jesus Christ on high.

The apostle proceeds to his perception of the saints and faithful brethren at Colosse, Ch. 1:3-8. This was a cause of thanksgiving to Paul and Timotheus. Hence—note carefully—consonant with the essential truth laid on his heart in the epistle to the Colossians. He says, 'We give thanks to God and the Father of our Lord Jesus Christ', 1:3.

If to the 'God' of our Lord Jesus Christ—for so the Greek reads—it follows that Christ is here considered in terms of Manhood. Yet, since he is described as 'Lord Jesus Christ', it is equally certain that ascended Manhood is in view, for this title is not used except to describe the Lord Jesus in his ascended glory, seated at the right hand of the Majesty on high.

Notwithstanding the ascension and glory of Christ, invisible in the heavens, mankind still continues unchanged upon the earth: but this is the old man, the carnal man, the worldly man, the first man, man of the earth, earthy, of the old Adam. To this earthy man pertains time and the present world. But his is a manhood under sin and sentence of death, and, withal, pending nothing save the end of the world, the resurrection of the unjust, and the judgment to come.

Then it follows of necessity that the new, risen Manhood which is in Christ, raised from the dead, ascended into heaven, which is the very embodiment of divine righteousness and life, is that manhood which has taken, and will take, the place of the first, earthly, man, in the purpose of God in the world to come.

For it is most evident that the Man seated in the glory, the Man at rest in the very presence of the Highest, must be possessed of Manhood of another order altogether. He is named, and named of God, both Lord and Christ, from the glorious heights of heaven.

He is called the firstborn, the firstbegotten from the dead, the beginning of the—new—creation of God. He is the Second Man, the last Adam, the life-giving spirit, the new Man, the heavenly Man, to whom pertains the everlasting glory, and the world to come, whereof we speak.

Furthermore, we are to observe that Paul and Timotheus not only gave thanks to God as the God of this New Man, to whom pertains the new Creation, but to God 'and the Father' of our Lord Jesus Christ. And if to the 'Father', then for the 'Son'.

But, whilst this thanksgiving of necessity includes his eternal Sonship in deity which he had with the Father before the world was, in such a context it was not exclusive to it. This thanksgiving was in terms of both what the Son is, and where the Son is, subsequent to his incarnation, death, resurrection, and ascension.

So that in giving thanks to God and the Father of our Lord Jesus Christ, the apostles not only had in mind all that the Son had done on earth, from the incarnation to the resurrection. That was included, but it was not the principal focus. The principal focus was *what* he is, and *where* he is, as ascended into glory.

The days of his flesh on earth were the days of his humiliation, days which had their conclusion in his being numbered with the transgressors, of his taking that flesh in which he had become incarnate, that manhood, down into death. Three days he lay in the grave. But the third day God raised him from the dead. That is, bodily. In that same body, raised from the dead, to die no more. Risen the other side of death, he was seen alive of chosen witnesses for forty days.

Then—and it cannot be overstressed: in that same body— he ascended into heaven. Henceforward, from the ascension, the full glory of the Son breaks forth, and breaks forth through that very same manhood in which he had suffered such degradation and humiliation at the hands of men on earth.

But, now glorified, for the first time it becomes manifest who is the blessed and only Potentate, the King of kings, and Lord of lords, who only hath immortality, dwelling in the light which no man can approach unto, whom no man hath seen, nor can see.

It was the chosen apostle Paul who was arrested on the Damascus road by the beams which shone from the countenance of the glorified Son, and who heard the voice of his mouth from heaven. From the light of this glory Paul remained blind for three days. Years later John also saw his face brighter than the sun in his strength and fell at his feet as dead. Thus the effulgent and unique manhood of the Son appears from the glory of the ascension in divine and heavenly radiance. But— and it cannot be stressed enough—this divine revelation shone forth from that same unique Manhood.

Yes, but now a hidden mystery comes to light. As Eve was taken out of Adam, so a bride appears in Christ, of his body, of his flesh, and of his bones. This is a great mystery, but I speak concerning Christ and the church. Henceforward the ascended Son, the Lord Jesus Christ, takes the place of glorified Head of a new order of heavenly manhood to be brought in by the Father according to the image of his own dear Son.

This once dead, three days buried, then raised, now glorified, ascended Manhood of the Son is declared from the resurrection day itself: 'In that he hath raised up Jesus again; as it is written in the second psalm, Thou art my Son, this day have I begotten thee'—that is, begotten from the dead—Acts 13:33.

And again, comparing the risen and ascended Manhood of the Son—and the Son in risen and ascended Manhood— comparing this, I say, with the nature and place of angels, God and the Father says of the Son, 'He hath by inheritance' —not by inherent deity, but by that inherent deity having taken manhood down into death, up into resurrection, and thence to the throne of his Father in glory—'He hath by inheritance obtained a more excellent name than they', that is, than the angels, Heb. 1:4.

Now here is the essence of Colossians distilled at the very commencement. Immediately this sets before the saints the hope of the gospel. For this is the hope of the gospel.

Having given thanks to God and the Father of our Lord Jesus Christ, to this the apostle joins continual prayer— 'praying always', Col. 1:3.

He gives thanks for their faith in Christ Jesus, and love to all the saints, deeply conscious that such inwrought faith and love can spring from nothing but the gift of the grace of God and the Father; and, being freely bestowed for no cause other than his own favour and loving-kindness, this evokes the deepest thanksgiving from the heart of the apostle.

But faith and love are neither enough of themselves, nor are they intended to subsist alone. Hence he prays for hope, 1:5. This hope is laid up in heaven, personified in the heavenly Man, and is declared in the word of the truth of the gospel.

Again and again, in one form or another, the apostle presses —as he prays for—the hope of the gospel in relation to the Colossians. This hope was in another Man, a world to come, a future realm of the inheritance of the saints in light, to be brought in when the earthy man, the present world, and this realm of darkness and death were no more.

Paul speaks of hope in Ch. 1:5; of patience—waiting for the hope—in 1:11; of longsuffering—enduring for the hope—again in Ch. 1:11; of the inheritance—the substance of the hope—in 1:12. Again he speaks of hope Ch. 1:23; and once more this is reiterated, Ch. 1:27.

Why so often? Because the Colossians were to see their deliverance in Christ from the entire old Creation; from the whole realm of the heavens and earth that now exist; from the complete sphere of the old man Adam, the man of the earth, earthy, destined by way of sin to return to the dust of death; from the total hierarchy of principalities, powers, lordships and dominions, visible and invisible, in heaven and earth, now pertaining to time: Delivered!

Out of and quite beyond all, reserved in Christ to an inheritance incorruptible and undefiled, destined for the world to come. That was their hope. It was what was declared in the word of the truth of the gospel. And that they might gain an interior spiritual grasp of it, by revelation and in experience, Paul laboured and travailed in prayer constantly.

And yet he had never met them. But this is the true ministry, and both Paul and Timotheus show the true office of minister.

The source of the apostle's perception of the Colossians' state came from the earnest labours of Epaphras, who was for them a faithful minister of Christ, whom Paul and Timotheus counted as a dear fellowservant. Epaphras was a living witness, in whom and by whom Paul received the testimony of the Spirit to the experiences and conditions of the saints at Colosse.

Receiving this twofold witness, confirmed by his own prophetic insight and spiritual perception, Paul's unfeigned thanksgiving and prayer joined with that of his true Colossian yokefellow, Epaphras, always labouring fervently for them in prayers, that they might stand perfect and complete in all the will of God.

And for this very reason Epaphras had come to Paul at Rome, unburdening his heart and spirit, and, in the will of God, thereby providing the occasion for the writing of an epistle blessed beyond all that either he or Paul could think, to the understanding, enlightenment, edification, and establishment of countless thousands of saints, even from generation to generation, to the latest day, reaching so far as to this present hour.

The apostle continues in thanksgiving that the word of the truth of the gospel—mark the description, Col. 1:5—had gone forth into all the world, and brought forth fruit, as it had done also in—observe that: in—the Colossians, since the day they heard of it, and knew the grace of God in truth—again, note the description—which they had also learned of Epaphras, the apostle's dear fellow-servant, and their faithful minister, who had declared to Paul their love in the Spirit.

For this cause, since the day Paul and Timotheus heard it, they ceased not to pray for them. That is, from the first day that they had heard that the Colossians had fruitfully received, known, and learned the word of the truth of the gospel, the grace of God in truth, so as to love and long after the apostles and their ministry in the Spirit.

However this ceaseless apostolic prayer was not made in vague, subjective, or emotional terms—God forbid—but in terms of the word of truth, the gospel of their salvation. He prays for them to be filled with the knowledge—mark that, the knowledge—of God's will in all wisdom—again note: All wisdom—and spiritual understanding—observe carefully: spiritual understanding—Col. 1:9.

In no other way—absolutely no other way—could the Colossians walk worthy of the Lord unto all pleasing, so as to be fruitful in every good work. The consequence of this however, would be increase: but increase not in the effect, but the cause: that is, increase in the knowledge of God. Nothing else would strengthen them.

But this, in proportion, order, and balance, certainly would strengthen them with all might, according to his glorious power, unto all patience and longsuffering with joyfulness.

Accordingly, abounding in the knowledge of God—Father, Son, and Holy Ghost—they would come to the spiritual perception of divine persons, the awareness of divine relationships, and the experimental knowledge of the work of Father, Son, and Holy Ghost distinctly.

Thus the Colossians would discern what it was to know God as Father, and how much they owed to God as their Father.

This awareness, spiritually communicated and experimentally received, would result in the outflowing of continual thanksgiving and praise to the Father in and of himself: 'Giving thanks unto the Father', Col. 1:12.

So much that is distinctive is owed to the Father, as the Son declares, 'My Father worketh hitherto, and I work'. All was through the Son, but all was from the Father. The saints were to know and feel that it was the Father himself who had made them meet for glory.

Everything already had been accomplished by the Father, through the Son, before they existed. They were saved before they were called, 'Who hath saved us—*first*—and called us—*second*—with an holy calling, not according to our works, but according to his own purpose and grace, which was given us in Christ Jesus before the world began', II Tim. 1:9.

They were called into that salvation to which the Father had chosen them. They were called into that salvation which the Father had already outwrought for them.

Truly, all had been done through the Son, but it had been done by the Father through the Son. And done on their behalf before they had so much as seen the light of day. The Father had done it all: how much they owed him! They owed him thanks for eternity.

It was he, the Father, which had made—it is in the past tense: 'hath made'—made them meet to be partakers of the inheritance of the saints in light. He had made them meet, past tense; for glory; future tense.

This past work, into the good of which they had been called, entailed the Father having already delivered them from the god of this world, as from the world itself: indeed, from the entire realm and age of the authority of darkness. Because this world, this age, was darkness. But the Father already had delivered them. Just as he had already translated them.

'And *hath* translated us into the kingdom of his dear Son', Col. 1:13. Paul is saying that the Father had done this on behalf of the Colossians, and that the thing was effected in the past tense before they were called. In his counsel and purpose, they were already in the glory. Thus they were as certain of that kingdom as was his own dear Son through whom the Father had secured it for them. Read Col. 1:12,13.

In the dear Son of the Father, by his grace, they had redemption through his blood, the forgiveness of sins. Not that they had the possibility of redemption. They had redemption. Not that the forgiveness of sins was available for them. They had the forgiveness of sins. The blood of God's dear Son in and of itself had already redeemed them, and had already secured their forgiveness. This was that into which they had been called by the gospel. It *is* the gospel!

Now Paul comes to the greatness of the person of the Son; still, remark, giving thanks to the Father. The apostle proceeds immediately to the power and glory of the person of the Son in the nature of his divinity, not in relation to the incarnation, but, spanning the ages of time before it, to the Creation.

Why? Because the apostle is to show the immense, the omnipotent, the almighty power—not to say the effectual reconciliation—essential to the bringing in of a new creation, the revelation of the riches of the glory of God's inheritance in the saints, and the creation of a new heavens, and a new earth, with a new divine administration and governmental order.

The establishment of these things yet to come is committed to the Son, being within his competence and his unique powers of performance. This is demonstrably true from all that he himself had framed from nothing at the beginning: 'Thou, Lord, in the beginning hast laid the foundation of the earth, and the heavens are the works of thy hands', Heb. 1:10.

It is evidently proven—this ability of his to create and bring in the inheritance of the world to come—by all that he had sustained and sustains even now by his word alone throughout the entire present heavens and earth who 'Upholdeth all things by the word of his power'. And, if so with the old, how much more with the new?

He is more than equal to dissolving all that he had created and made, has sustained, and still sustains, from the beginning, till the end, until he frames anew that world which is to come according to the good pleasure of his will, and the fulfilment of God's eternal purpose in grace.

It is to bring out this evident proof and demonstration of the power and authority of the Son, already fully made manifest in the creation of the heavens and the earth in the beginning of the world, that the apostle now writes, 1:15,16.

Why? Because he purposes to set before the Colossians the hope of the gospel in the creation of a new heavens and a new earth when this present world is no more.

Clearly therefore such a hope depends upon the Son being equal to so immeasurable a task: Can he do it? He can not only do it, but, in the creation that now exists, he has already done it.

Now the apostle launches upon a revelation of the divine person, authority, and power of the Son, showing proof positive that he is more than able to bring in the glorious inheritance of the saints in light, when this present shameful age of darkness and death has passed into oblivion for ever.

This is the hope of the gospel. And, to a demonstration, the Son is equal to its fulfilment.

Demonstrably the Son is more than equal to bringing in the hope of the gospel at the last day, for he has already done as much in the creation of the world on the first day. Evidently he is as equal to establishing divine government, visible and invisible, in the new heavens and new earth, as he was in establishing the principalities, powers, thrones, and dominions in the heavens and earth that are now.

What he had done in the first day, he can certainly do in the last. What he did in the old creation, he is more than able to do in the new.

The meanwhile it is evident that he sustains—and will sustain—with sublime power, all that he had created and made in the heavens above and in the earth beneath, over the vast arc of the ages from the first day until the last, till time shall be no more, and the saints shall be raised in light to their glorious and eternal inheritance.

That is why the apostle proceeds from 'Redemption through his blood, even the forgiveness of sins', 1:14, immediately to the almighty and invincible power and authority of the Son in the Creation and in its subsistence throughout time, 1:15-17.

However, we are to observe that the terms, Col. 1:15, 'the image of the invisible God', and 'the firstborn of every creature', distinctly speak of the Son *as Man*.

This is not to focus on the days of the humiliation of the Son of man, the days from the incarnation to the grave, when 'he was made a little lower than the angels for the suffering of death'. Those were 'the days of his flesh', when he was tempted in all points like as we are, yet without sin. That was the time on earth when, though he were a Son, yet learned he obedience by the things which he suffered, who, being made perfect, became the author of eternal salvation unto them that obey him.

This is rather to emphasize his Manhood from the resurrection and in the ascension, in which he is seen as Head of a new order, begotten in himself, by himself, from himself, and after his own image.

This is Manhood in the Son, and of the Son, raised from the dead, and seated in glory. This is the new order of Man in sonship, heavenly, mysterious, spiritual, and divine: after himself, the image of the invisible God, and in himself, begotten out of the dead.

The Head is unique: the members are in him, and from him, and by him in due order: Christ the firstfruits, then afterwards they that are Christ's at his coming. First, inwardly in life; finally, outwardly in resurrection.

His ability—almighty and irresistible—to fulfil the divine purpose, to change the living, to raise the sons of God from the dust of death, to create a new heaven and a new earth, to bring in the glory—as the apostle demonstrates—having been proven and foreshadowed in his forming from absolutely nothing the whole old order, and the entire first creation.

The Creation did not, and does not, run itself, neither is it maintained by laws without lawgivers, nor does it function without functionaries, much less is it administered without a due order of governmental stratum in that administration.

These serried ranks of government, these seats of ascending authority, these ranks of administration, these offices of due order, in and of themselves are called 'things', Col. 1:16,17.

But all these 'things', from the very commencement, from the first beginning, even from the foundation of the world, were created by him. Not then in ascended Manhood as Son. Then in eternal deity as Son.

Nevertheless, the Son, himself, created all 'things': in heaven, on earth, visible, invisible, whether thrones, dominions, principalities, or powers, all 'things' were created by him and for him.

And, of course, the eternal Son was before all 'things' in almighty power, divine being, inscrutable deity, eternal relationships, everlasting glory, and absolute authority.

Moreover, not only did he form such offices to be filled by created beings at his will, they subsist by him: ever since, 'he upholdeth all things by the word of his power'.

That there has been war in heaven, and ruin on earth, alters none of this. It is a question of the offices which he ordained, and which he administers, by absolute authority, as he ever did, as he does, and as he will do till the end of the world.

The end of the world: and then? Then the inheritance, the world to come, which, seeing the vastness of his being, the invincibility of his power, and the mystery of his person, it is abundantly evident, he is more than able to bring in for the glory of the Father. If so, in Sonship. Then, by resurrection. Therefore, having accomplished redemption. Hence, as bringing in reconciliation.

This is even now seen in an utterly new, entirely spiritual, yet visibly united mystery: his body.

He is the Head of the body, the church; the *ecclesia*: the beginning—before his members were yet formed, Ps. 139:16—the firstborn from the dead.

In everything he is first: he is pre-eminent. It was pleasing that in him should all the fulness dwell: that is, all is in him, all is from him, and all is by him, who is the fountain of life in the resurrection from the dead.

He made peace by the blood of his cross, 1:20, that is, the Head for all the members, as yet hidden in him. When these, the elect, were called, they were called into a peace which he had already secured, and which he had afore ratified, by his own blood.

Then what must be the destiny of such a body as this, for whom he made peace at so great a price as his own blood? They were predestinated to be conformed to the image of God's dear Son, and, if so, their destiny must be the inheritance of the world to come. But if of the world to come, what of all 'things' in the world that now is?

As 'things'—not as the beings which occupy them—these are reconciled, whether they be 'things' in heaven, or 'things' on earth. 'All things', that is, in terms of seats of government, and offices of administration, hath he reconciled unto himself.

The exalted occupants have not overcome him, as they thought: he has overcome them, as they thought not. Why did they think not? Because they had a right on their side. They held their offices by his appointment; and they ruled the world under his authority. They knew that he would neither overturn authority, nor be inconsistent with the order that he had appointed over the world.

But at the cross, in effect, he has ended the world: 'Now is the judgment of this world: now shall the prince of this world be cast out', Jn. 12:31. 'But now once in the end of the world hath he appeared to put away sin by the sacrifice of himself', Heb. 9:26.

But what of the future? A glorious inheritance. By what government? The same offices, but new incumbents. But who will inherit? He must inherit, who is appointed heir of all things, Heb. 1:2.

Will he inherit alone? No; in him, and with him, appears every heir of promise, the entire *huiothesia*, every son begotten in him and by him, raised from the dead at his appearing; and all his holy angels with him.

All things in Christ. That is not just the prospect: it is the inevitable consequence of his glorious work; the absolute certainty of the future; to which his mighty power is more than equal.

Hence reconciliation is twofold: by redemption and by authority; in the past tense and in the future; of persons and of things. Headship also is twofold: he is Head of the body, and he is Head of all things; Head over all things in creation, Head of the body in new creation.

Likewise the ministry which flows from him by his ordina-tion and authority: it is of the gospel preached to every creature, and it is of the body according to the fellowship of the mystery; it is preached among the Gentiles, it is taught in the house of God.

Twofold: two creations; two circumcisions; two baptisms; two men: yes, but it is the spiritual which overcomes the natural; the heavenly which transcends the earthly; the inward which subdues the outward.

Blessed are they whose eyes behold, and whose ears hear, the mystery of godliness now revealed, for without controversy great is the mystery of godliness.

Thus Paul makes known by this epistle the riches of the glory of this mystery among the Gentiles, 'which is Christ in you, the hope of glory'.

Observe, 1:27, it is Christ in 'you'—not in 'thee'. It is the indwelling of Christ in the whole body, not in isolated indi-viduals. Not even unity manifested together at Colosse only, but at Colosse as manifesting the unity of the entire assembly. This is the oneness that each and every assembly manifested as constituting *the* assembly on earth.

Again, 'Christ in you' indicates what we are for him: not what he is for us. It is what the *ecclesia* is for him. It is his body.

He dwells therein. In the unity of all in each place, with all in every place, his one dwelling place appears.

Nevertheless, from the warnings of the Lord Jesus in the gospels, by the experience of the apostles in the event, nothing could be taken for granted. God's election was sure, but man's profession was not.

Many could go, and did go, so far in appearance: 'who were once enlightened, and had tasted of the heavenly gift, and were made partakers of the Holy Ghost, and had tasted of the good word of God, and the powers of the world to come'—so far—and yet they fell away at the last. This was experience, not theory: it had happened, it was happening, and it would happen again.

Hence, for all the certainty of God's foundation, the immutability of his counsel, the unconditional nature of his salvation, the everlasting certainty of his election, the assured endurance of all the chosen of God, in practice the apostle issued the sternest of warnings of the inevitable consequences of continuing in sin, walking in the flesh, or persevering in error.

Error was no mark of the elect. But it was a mark of many who afterwards fell away, yet had begun in a way that appeared identical with the elect.

Hence the apostolic labours, striving in prayer, with many tears, to present every man perfect in Christ Jesus, and, in righteousness, to expose, rebuke, and correct error at the slightest hint of its appearance, tempering all comfort with this warning: '*If* ye continue in the faith grounded and settled, and be not moved away from the hope of the gospel', 1:23.

The apostle will not be blinded by outward appearances: he allows of no presumption. Ever vigilant, he is alert to all the wiles of the adversary. Constantly he is on guard against the corruption of the flesh, the enmity of the carnal mind, the powers of darkness above, the depth of blackness below, and the multitude of afflictions ahead.

The apostle warns continually that the saints' pathway lies through much tribulation, in an age swarming and populated with bitter and deadly enemies, subtle temptations, many seducers, and a host of false teachers.

Through all these things the saints must pass, and yet be kept in holiness and righteousness, in spiritual and experimental continuance in the truth of the gospel, sustained and nurtured under the faithful labours of true gospel ministers, in the one unity of the assembly, which is his body, the fulness of him that filleth all in all.

Hence Paul declares his ministry, both in the gospel, and to the body, with all the heart-breaking afflictions which this entailed.

His labours and travails were to this end: that they might stand perfect in one, bound together in love, increasing in the knowledge of God, and holding fast the word of the truth of the gospel.

Paul's desire was to see the Colossians united with all saints in the fellowship of the mystery, in one body, in the full knowledge of the Son of God, complete in Christ, and holding fast the Head.

This was the purpose of his ministry, and the end of this present letter. So he labours for them. The more so because subtle errors existed, and subtler men to insinuate them, to deflect the minds of the weak, and overthrow the faith of some.

Therefore the apostle strenuously asserts that all wisdom is in Christ, and, moreover, must be conveyed experimentally by the Father and the Son from above.

Nothing is outside of Christ; nothing can communicate Christ but the power of God; and nothing exists in man whereby he can lay hold of these divine things: it is they that must lay hold of him, and, if so, the initiative must be of God. Help is in his power alone, and granted by nothing but his own grace.

So the servant of Christ, Paul, affirms, greatly desiring their increase, labouring in prayer on their behalf, lest in any way they should be beguiled from the simplicity that is in Christ, either by Jewish legalities or Gentile philosophies.

All the wisdom of God was in Christ, and this God retained in his own prerogative to dispose and dispense by grace according to his own will: yes, but blessed be God, they were found in Christ. Then let them take heed, and abide therein in the fear of God, for this was all the desire of the apostle, Ch. 1:9 to Ch. 2:5.

From Ch. 2:6 through to Ch. 4:6 Paul commands the obedience of faith, first laying down the foundation of sound doctrine, 2:6-15.

Certainly they had received Christ Jesus the Lord. But as the Lord had said, 'If ye continue in my word, then are ye my disciples indeed; and ye shall know the truth, and the truth shall make you free', Jn. 8:30-32.

So saith the apostle, 'As ye have therefore received Christ Jesus the Lord, so walk ye in him: rooted and built up in him, and stablished in the faith, as ye have been taught, abounding therein with thanksgiving', Col. 2:6,7.

But they were to be vigilant: 'Beware lest any man spoil you', 2:8. Spoil them? Yes, with perverse disputings; legal wranglings; flattering speeches; fair words; loose corruption; intriguing philosophy; traditional theology; in a word, summing up what is contrary to sound doctrine according to the glorious gospel, 'philosophy and vain deceit, after the tradition of men, after the rudiments of the world, and not after Christ', 2:8.

Now, according to the glorious gospel of the blessed God, committed to the apostle's trust, the fulness of the Godhead dwelt bodily in Christ, Col. 2:9. Then, nowhere else. All else was darkness: in heaven, on earth; visible, or invisible; in the world, throughout time.

All that was of God—his fulness, the fulness of the Godhead —dwelt bodily in Christ, and in him they were complete.

Nothing else existed for the saints anywhere else: not in Adam; not in the flesh; not in the world; not in time: they were complete, absolutely complete, in Christ.

In him they were circumcised (though not in an outward or material way of the flesh) through the putting off of the body of the sin—it is not 'sins' in the Greek, nor could it be; the translators err: it is 'sin'—of the flesh. The whole body of sin had been circumcised, cut round, cut off, cast away: that had happened for them in Christ at the cross, and, in the doctrine, they were to walk in the light of it.

So baptism: Christ had gone down into the waters of death for them, and in him they were risen for ever beyond its power: beyond death; the grave; man alive in this world; the entire present age: dead to it all, and inwardly risen with him to the hope of the gospel.

This was their calling, and it was by whole-hearted submission to the sound doctrine of those sent to preach and teach it that they should live.

They were called into all that the Father had wrought for them in the Son. They did not do the calling, any more than the working. How could they? They had been 'dead in their sins, and the uncircumcision of their flesh', 2:13. Dead men, much less in filth wholly obnoxious to the wrath of God, cannot 'accept the gospel offer' or 'let Jesus in': dead men can do nothing but putrify.

But God, for his great love wherewith he loved them, had quickened them together with Christ out of death.

This was God's work, and into it they were called, into this faith, believing what God had done, who had united them to Christ, at the cross, in death, through resurrection, and into glory. If so, they were called, and called inwardly of God, according to the glorious gospel of the blessed God.

As to principalities and powers and the like, angels withal, that were of the darkness of this world, they were spoiled. The fall of man had been their rise; the sin of man their establishment; the death of man their glory; and the law given to men their strength: 'The strength of sin is the law', I Cor. 15:56.

This side of death the law of commandments contained in ordinances was both immutable and inexorable. As alive in this world, the law bound, yoked, condemned, and cursed men. So long as they remained living upon the face of the earth, the law was against them, and contrary to them. There was no deliverance from it, yet they could never keep it. It cursed men to death, and after death was the judgment. Hence, through fear of death, because of the law, all their lifetime they were subject to bondage.

But the Father sent the Son, the Son took the law of commandments contained in ordinances, and he nailed it to his cross. Moreover he brought us by that cross into death, through the grave, by resurrection, into the glorious liberty and inheritance of the hope of the gospel.

Alive beyond death, where was the law? Nailed to the cross in this present world where man was alive in the flesh.

But the saints were dead. They were not reckoned to be in the flesh. The law could not then—nor can it for eternity—be brought over the great gulf fixed by the finality of death.

Death was the final sentence, the ultimate demand, and the last word of the law.

Death satisfied each lawful demand and every legal sanction. It also took all the authority out of the hands of principalities and powers, leaving them stupified and helpless. Thus Christ delivered us, made an open show of them, the meanwhile magnifying the law and making it honourable.

This took the elect beyond the reach of the law, beyond all that God had to say in the old testament to man alive in the flesh, beyond the rudiments of the world, past all shadows.

Then why regard them? Meats; drinks; holy days; feasts of the week or month; the sabbath: all shadows. But now the substance had come, and the saints were in it, and of it: the new testament being that of our Lord and Saviour Jesus Christ.

The saints were not to let men beguile them. God never sent such men, though they came in droves and arrived in swarms, with never so many pretensions and high-sounding claims, blowing the trumpet and sounding the brass of what was no more than the light and airy assumption of authority from man.

Receive them not. Neither regard, no, nor even hear their enticing words, which of necessity are contrary to sound doctrine according to the glorious gospel of the blessed God committed to the trust of those whom God commands and Christ sends.

Having laid down his doctrine, the apostle admonishes the Colossians, Ch. 2:16-19. His exhortation follows, 2:20 to 4:6.

The very essence of the saints' position in Christ in the Epistle to the Colossians appears in Ch. 3:1-3, where the apostle draws from the doctrine to press home his exhortation.

The doctrine states what has been accomplished by the Father and the Son through the death and resurrection of Christ not for himself alone but for all his members. If he died, they died. If he rose, they rose.

Into this position wrought for them by the Father and the Son, the saints are called by grace. Inwardly the power of God supports this position according to the faith freely bestowed and given by grace to the hidden man of the heart.

Outwardly, the flesh is still unchanged; the world is still unchanged; and time is still unchanged. Inwardly, however, faith is to triumph over all, and overcome all, so as to credit the entire work of Christ, dwelling in it, appropriating it, walking in it.

This is called, The work of faith with power. The flesh militates against this, the law knows nothing of it, the world derides it, and the carnal mind contends against so triumphant a faith with murmuring and bitter enmity.

But what of it? That was all crucified in Christ, and if so, it is to be mortified, denied, refused, ignored, and turned from by the interior man, whom God upholds in this mortification, supporting the saints inwardly in heart to walk by faith, strengthened with all might according to his glorious power.

But if dead, then risen. 'If ye then be risen with Christ', 3:1. That is the doctrine. When Christ rose, all his elect rose in him. In process of time they are called. That is, called by the voice of the Son of God into this very same gospel.

The voice of the Son speaks within of having already obtained eternal redemption for his people; of his having now achieved everlasting reconciliation on their behalf; of unconditional salvation having been effectually outwrought by the blood of his cross in their stead.

And as, within, Christ testifies of all that he had before accomplished in death, the Spirit bears witness with the doctrine taught in the gospel of the grace of Christ, the gospel of God concerning his Son.

Faith, the gift of God within the saints, credits the truth of this gospel in its entirety. Faith stands to the doctrine. Now comes the exhortation: 'If'—observe the force and the directness of the apostle's application—'If ye then be risen with Christ, seek those things which are above, where Christ sitteth on the right hand of God.'

Christ has taken the saints through death, and up into life from the other side of death. That is the doctrine. Their experience, whom he calls, answers to this: having believed, they have life in his name.

That life is eternal: it is everlasting life. It flows from the resurrection and ascension of the Son of God. It comes from him who sits in the heavenly glory, for ever the other side, the Jordan side, the glory side, the eternity side of death.

Everlasting life beyond the reach of death fills the saints and testifies to the truth of the doctrine of Christ: they rose when he rose. 'If ye then be risen with Christ'—then—'set your affections on things above, not on things on the earth', 3:2.

The earth with its things is still there. But the faith rises over all. Carnality with its corruptions is still active. But faith appropriates the place that Christ took at the cross on one's behalf, and reckons all dead, despite the clamour of the flesh for the attention of the soul.

Dwelling in Christ within, inwardly in the life, all the carnality of the flesh, all the things on the earth to which the flesh corresponds, all are resolutely denied: mortified.

Neither the flesh nor the things of the earth are dead to us; no, but we are dead to it and to them, and, already, within, are risen in newness of life. In this we dwell, and by this set our affections on the heavenly Son in the glory, his God our God, and his Father our Father.

Of course we are dead: we died when he died. This did not happen to us: it happened to him.

But it is conveyed to us, and, receiving the doctrine, despite the activity of the world; the presence of the things of the earth; the carnal enmity of the flesh; and the continued existence of time, we believe God, we believe in Christ, and we reckon ourselves dead to all, whilst we wait for God's Son from heaven to change this vile body and to end this dark world.

'When Christ, who is our life'—that is, our life now, within, dwelling in us, and we in him, in the interior man: our life— 'When Christ, who is our life, shall appear, then shall ye also appear with him in glory', Col. 3:4.

The exhortation continues: 'Therefore'. On this account. On account of our having died with Christ. Of our having risen with him when he rose.

Mortify 'therefore', by that inwardly given but actually risen life. For the life is within, but the flesh and its members are without.

'Mortify therefore your members which are upon the earth.' Not as do those blinded fanatics who mortify the physical members. These are not physical members. 'Your members which are upon the earth; fornication, uncleanness, inordinate affection, evil concupiscence, and covetousness, which is idolatry.'

These are not physical members. They come from within. Nevertheless, none of these members is in the life, and the life is in none of these members.

But we are in the life, and the life is in us, and, since the life is risen, and we rose in the life, by that life, in the power of it, we are to mortify such members whilst waiting for the coming of Christ, knowing that when Christ, who is our life, shall appear, then shall we also appear with him in glory.

Waiting, that is, according to his glorious power, daily strengthening us within, standing by, supporting, giving credence to the apostles' doctrine, namely, the doctrine of Christ.

By this, through faith, we are to put off the old man, separating our inward life from that man, whilst putting on the new man, who is 'renewed in knowledge after the image of him that created him', Col. 3:10.

The new man is over all that is of the earth, or after the flesh. Of course: this new man rose from the dead, where all distinctions cease, and the life of the flesh is extinguished. But we are quickened, created anew, to dwell in the life of the Son of God in a mystery, namely, Christ in us the hope of glory.

But what kind of image is that of the new man, in which image we are renewed in knowledge after the likeness of him which created him?

This interior, heavenly, spiritual, new-created Man bears the glorious likeness of the risen Son, who is the image of the invisible God, the brightness of his glory, the express image of his person. This the elect of God, holy and beloved, put on, just as by the same faith and power they put off the old.

Now they appear in another, glorious, light: bowels of mercies; kindness; humbleness of mind; meekness; longsuffering; forbearance of one another; full of forgiveness; bound within and girt about with perfect love; filled with the peace of God. Called into one body. Thankful.

The word of Christ dwells in this new man, this inward man, this spiritual man, this man of faith, richly in all wisdom, as each teaches and admonishes the other in psalms and hymns and spiritual songs—that is, the Psalms, Hymns, and Spiritual Songs, *meant by the apostle**—singing with grace in the heart to the Lord.

The apostle proceeds in his exhortation to relationships entailed in the saints' pathway through this present but passing world, describing how the gospel of Christ directs them to walk in every case.

He applies this truth to the relationship of wives to husbands; husbands to wives; children to parents; fathers to children; servants to masters; masters to servants. Whatever the relationship may be, and in whatsoever circumstances, the new man acts therein, and walks by grace through faith, so as to adorn the doctrine of God our Saviour in all things.

The saints' pilgrimage demands continual prayer and constant watchfulness, and to this end the apostle fervently exhorts the brethren.

---

*See 'The Psalms of the Old Testament', 'The Hymns of the New Testament', and 'Spiritual Songs from the Gospels', by John Metcalfe; available from The Publishing Trust.

He beseeches prayer for himself and Timotheus, that God would open unto them a door of utterance to speak the mystery of Christ, for which he was also in bonds: that he might make this mystery manifest, as he ought to speak.

And how much more was this both necessary and urgent, now that the world was swarming with airy and light opportunists, capitalizing on the spread of the word, destitute of the truth, void of the least work of God, corrupters of the gospel, having neither the power, nor the anointing.

Paul speaks of wisdom in maintaining separation from these, as from the apostasy, and from the world. Likewise of redeeming the time; so much time had been lost: so little remained.

As to their speech, it should be always—mark that, always —with grace, seasoned with salt. That is, the salt of the covenant, a sharp astringent sprinkling of which should overlay all the assembled words of grace issuing forth in speech from the mouth.

By this they should know how they ought to answer every man in all circumstances.

Finally, Ch. 4:7-18, Paul proposes the love of the brethren. Not of the world. Not of the flesh. Not of the neighbour. Exclusively of the brethren, begotten of the Father, quickened by the Son, having the same life, eternal life, from the Head of the body in the heavenly glory.

And more: divine life in new manhood. This made them brethren. This confirmed their salvation. This formed the union in the house of God not made with hands.

Such brotherly love, seen in the salutations with which the epistle closes, comes—and could only come—from one source. From the Head in heaven. Therein lay their union, thence was their life, therefrom their nourishment, and hence their brotherhood.

In such bonds of love, by such a union of love, by such salutations of love, holding the Head was made manifest.

Not only in the union between themselves, but that between all saints alike gathered in every place. For there was one union, one fellowship, one brotherhood. One Spirit, one body, one hope of their calling; one Lord, one faith, one baptism; one God and Father of all, above all, through all, and in all.

Not simply all at Colosse: all in God the Father, and in the Lord Jesus Christ. One *ecclesia*. Their love to all the saints made this unity manifest, and made it manifest in Colosse, and from Colosse.

Thus appeared a union so divine, so heavenly, so spiritual, so mysterious. It was the visible evidence of their holding fast the Head, from which all the body by joints and bands having nourishment ministered, and knit together, increased with the increase of God.

The closing salutation is in Paul's own handwriting: it was not dictated. He wrote it himself. 'Remember my bonds', he entreats. 'Grace with you. Amen.' And this to brethren whom he had never seen in the flesh, and to a place to which he had never been on earth. Perhaps not, but his heart burned with love within him; his bent knees bore witness to his fervent travail in prayer on their behalf, as if they had been his own dearly beloved sons.

Finally his hand at rest, having laid down his pen, mute witness is borne to the finished epistle. Full of Christ, full of divinity, full of priceless truth, all reaching far beyond the Colossians.

Yes, reaching beyond that generation, reaching to age beyond age, wondrously preserved, until, translated, in this present day one takes up and reads these selfsame pages, radiant with a love to Christ, burning with a devotion to the purpose of God, and alive with a largeness of heart for all saints, more enduring than time itself.

And, never so inwardly, one seems to hear an echo, carried from ages and generations upon the winds of time, but sounding still: 'Remember my bonds. Grace be with you. Amen.'

JOHN METCALFE

INDEX

TO OTHER PUBLICATIONS

PSALMS, HYMNS AND SPIRITUAL SONGS

THE PSALMS

OF THE

OLD TESTAMENT

The Psalms of the Old Testament, the result of years of painstaking labour, is an original translation into verse from the Authorised Version, which seeks to present the Psalms in the purest scriptural form possible for singing. Here, for the first time, divine names are rendered as and when they occur in the scripture, the distinction between LORD and Lord has been preserved, and every essential point of doctrine and experience appears with unique perception and fidelity.

The Psalms of the Old Testament is the first part of a trilogy written by John Metcalfe, the second part of which is entitled *Spiritual Songs from the Gospels*, and the last, *The Hymns of the New Testament*. These titles provide unique and accurate metrical versions of passages from the psalms, the gospels and the new testament epistles respectively, and are intended to be used together in the worship of God.

Price £2.50 *(postage extra)*
(hard-case binding, dust-jacket)
Printed, sewn and bound
by the John Metcalfe Publishing Trust
ISBN 0 9506366 7 3

v

SPIRITUAL SONGS

FROM

THE GOSPELS

The *Spiritual Songs from the Gospels*, the result of years of painstaking labour, is an original translation into verse from the Authorised Version, which seeks to present essential parts of the gospels in the purest scriptural form possible for singing. The careful selection from Matthew, Mark, Luke and John, set forth in metrical verse of the highest integrity, enables the singer to sing 'the word of Christ' as if from the scripture itself, 'richly and in all wisdom'; and, above all, in a way that facilitates worship in song of unprecedented fidelity.

The *Spiritual Songs from the Gospels* is the central part of a trilogy written by John Metcalfe, the first part of which is entitled *The Psalms of the Old Testament*, and the last, *The Hymns of the New Testament*. These titles provide unique and accurate metrical versions of passages from the psalms, the gospels and the new testament epistles respectively, and are intended to be used together in the worship of God.

Price £2.50 *(postage extra)*
(hard-case binding, dust-jacket)
Printed, sewn and bound
by the John Metcalfe Publishing Trust
ISBN 0 9506366 8 1

THE HYMNS

OF THE

NEW TESTAMENT

The *Hymns of the New Testament*, the result of years of painstaking labour, is an original translation into verse from the Authorised Version, which presents essential parts of the new testament epistles in the purest scriptural form possible for singing. The careful selection from the book of Acts to that of Revelation, set forth in metrical verse of the highest integrity, enables the singer to sing 'the word of Christ' as if from the scripture itself, 'richly and in all wisdom'; and, above all, in a way that facilitates worship in song of unprecedented fidelity.

The *Hymns of the New Testament* is the last part of a trilogy written by John Metcalfe, the first part of which is entitled *The Psalms of the Old Testament*, and the next, *Spiritual Songs from the Gospels*. These titles provide unique and accurate metrical versions of passages from the psalms, the gospels and the new testament epistles respectively, and are intended to be used together in the worship of God.

Price £2.50 *(postage extra)*
(hard-case binding, dust-jacket)
Printed, sewn and bound
by the John Metcalfe Publishing Trust
ISBN 0 9506366 9 X

'THE APOSTOLIC FOUNDATION
OF THE
CHRISTIAN CHURCH' SERIES

Third Printing

FOUNDATIONS UNCOVERED

THE APOSTOLIC FOUNDATION
OF THE
CHRISTIAN CHURCH

Volume I

Foundations Uncovered is the introduction to the major series: 'The Apostolic Foundation of the Christian Church'.

Rich in truth, the Introduction deals comprehensively with the foundation of the apostolic faith under the descriptive titles: The Word, The Doctrine, The Truth, The Gospel, The Faith, The New Testament, and The Foundation.

The contents of the book reveal: The Fact of the Foundation; The Foundation Uncovered; What the Foundation is not; How the Foundation is Described; and, Being Built upon the Foundation.

'This book comes with the freshness of a new Reformation.'

Price 75p *(postage extra)*
(Laminated cover)
Printed, sewn and bound
by the John Metcalfe Publishing Trust
ISBN 0 9506366 5 7

Thoroughly revised and extensively rewritten
second edition

Third Printing

THE BIRTH OF JESUS CHRIST

THE APOSTOLIC FOUNDATION
OF THE
CHRISTIAN CHURCH

Volume II

'The very spirit of adoration and worship rings through the pages of *The Birth of Jesus Christ*.

'The author expresses with great clarity the truths revealed to him in his study of holy scriptures at depth. We are presented here with a totally lofty view of the Incarnation.

'John Metcalfe is to be classed amongst the foremost expositors of our age; and his writings have about them that quality of timelessness that makes me sure they will one day take their place among the heritage of truly great Christian works.'

From a review by Rev. David Catterson.

'Uncompromisingly faithful to scripture ... has much to offer which is worth serious consideration ... deeply moving.'

The Expository Times.

Price 95p *(postage extra)*
(Laminated Cover)
Printed, sewn and bound
by the John Metcalfe Publishing Trust
ISBN 1 870039 48 3

*Thoroughly revised and extensively rewritten
second edition*

Third Printing

THE MESSIAH

THE APOSTOLIC FOUNDATION
OF THE
CHRISTIAN CHURCH

Volume III

The Messiah is a spiritually penetrating and entirely original exposition of Matthew chapter one to chapter seven from the trenchant pen of John Metcalfe.

Matthew Chapters One to Seven

GENEALOGY · BIRTH · STAR OF BETHLEHEM
HEROD · FLIGHT TO EGYPT · NAZARETH
JOHN THE BAPTIST · THE BAPTIST'S MINISTRY
JESUS' BAPTISM · ALL RIGHTEOUSNESS FULFILLED
HEAVEN OPENED · THE SPIRIT'S DESCENT
THE TEMPTATION OF JESUS IN THE WILDERNESS
JESUS' MANIFESTATION · THE CALLING · THE TRUE DISCIPLES
THE BEATITUDES · THE SERMON ON THE MOUNT

'Something of the fire of the ancient Hebrew prophet .... Metcalfe has spiritual and expository potentials of a high order.'

The Life of Faith.

Price £7.75 *(postage extra)*
Hardback 420 pages
Laminated bookjacket
Printed, sewn and bound
by the John Metcalfe Publishing Trust
ISBN 1 870039 51 3

THE SON OF GOD AND SEED OF DAVID

THE APOSTOLIC FOUNDATION
OF THE
CHRISTIAN CHURCH

Volume IV

The Son of God and Seed of David is the fourth volume in the major work entitled 'The Apostolic Foundation of the Christian Church.'

'The author proceeds to open and allege that Jesus Christ is and ever was *The Son of God*. This greatest of subjects, this most profound of all mysteries, is handled with reverence and with outstanding perception.

'The second part considers *The Seed of David*. What is meant precisely by 'the seed'? And why 'of David'? With prophetic insight the author expounds these essential verities.'

Price £6.95 *(postage extra)*
Hardback 250 pages
Laminated bookjacket
Printed, sewn and bound
by the John Metcalfe Publishing Trust
ISBN 1 870039 16 5

CHRIST CRUCIFIED

THE APOSTOLIC FOUNDATION
OF THE
CHRISTIAN CHURCH

Volume V

Christ Crucified the definitive work on the crucifixion, the blood, and the cross of Jesus Christ.

The crucifixion of Jesus Christ witnessed in the Gospels: the gospel according to Matthew; Mark; Luke; John.

The blood of Jesus Christ declared in the Epistles: the shed blood; the blood of purchase; redemption through his blood; the blood of sprinkling; the blood of the covenant.

The doctrine of the cross revealed in the apostolic foundation of the Christian church: the doctrine of the cross; the cross and the body of sin; the cross and the carnal mind; the cross and the law; the offence of the cross; the cross of our Lord Jesus Christ.

Price £6.95 *(postage extra)*
Hardback 300 pages
Laminated bookjacket
Printed, sewn and bound
by the John Metcalfe Publishing Trust
ISBN 1 870039 08 4

JUSTIFICATION BY FAITH

THE APOSTOLIC FOUNDATION
OF THE
CHRISTIAN CHURCH

Volume VI

THE HEART OF THE GOSPEL · THE FOUNDATION OF THE CHURCH
THE ISSUE OF ETERNITY
CLEARLY, ORIGINALLY AND POWERFULLY OPENED

The basis · The righteousness of the law
The righteousness of God · The atonement · Justification
Traditional views considered · Righteousness imputed to faith
Faith counted for righteousness · Justification by Faith

'And it came to pass, when Jesus had ended these sayings, the people were astonished at his doctrine: for he taught them as one having authority, and not as the scribes.' Matthew 7:28,29.

Price £7.50 (*postage extra*)
Hardback 375 pages
Laminated bookjacket
Printed, sewn and bound
by the John Metcalfe Publishing Trust
ISBN 1870039 11 4

THE CHURCH: WHAT IS IT?

THE APOSTOLIC FOUNDATION
OF THE
CHRISTIAN CHURCH

Volume VII

The answer to this question proceeds first from the lips of Jesus himself, Mt. 16:18, later to be expounded by the words of the apostles whom he sent.

Neither fear of man nor favour from the world remotely affect the answer.

Here is the truth, the whole truth, and nothing but the truth.

The complete originality, the vast range, and the total fearlessness of this book command the attention in a way that is unique.

Read this book: you will never read another like it.

Outspokenly devastating yet devastatingly constructive.

Price £7.75 *(postage extra)*
Hardback 400 pages
Laminated bookjacket
Printed, sewn and bound
by the John Metcalfe Publishing Trust
ISBN 1 870039 23 8

OTHER TITLES

NOAH AND THE FLOOD

Noah and the Flood expounds with vital urgency the man and the message that heralded the end of the old world. The description of the flood itself is vividly realistic. The whole work has an unmistakable ring of authority, and speaks as 'Thus saith the Lord'.

'Mr. Metcalfe makes a skilful use of persuasive eloquence as he challenges the reality of one's profession of faith ... he gives a rousing call to a searching self-examination and evaluation of one's spiritual experience.'
The Monthly Record of the Free Church of Scotland.

Price £1.90 *(postage extra)*
(Laminated Cover)
Printed, sewn and bound
by the John Metcalfe Publishing Trust
ISBN 1 870039 22 X

DIVINE FOOTSTEPS

Divine Footsteps traces the pathway of the feet of the Son of man from the very beginning in the prophetic figures of the true in the old testament through the reality in the new; doing so in a way of experimental spirituality. At the last a glimpse of the coming glory is beheld as his feet are viewed as standing at the latter day upon the earth.

Price 95p *(postage extra)*
(Laminated Cover)
Printed, sewn and bound
by the John Metcalfe Publishing Trust
ISBN 1 870039 21 1

THE RED HEIFER

The Red Heifer was the name given to a sacrifice used by the children of Israel in the Old Testament—as recorded in Numbers 19—in which a heifer was slain and burned. Cedar wood, hyssop and scarlet were cast into the burning, and the ashes were mingled with running water and put in a vessel. It was kept for the children of Israel for a water of separation: it was a purification for sin.

In this unusual book the sacrifice is brought up to date and its relevance to the church today is shown.

Price 75p *(postage extra)*
ISBN 0 9502515 4 2

THE WELLS OF SALVATION

The Wells of Salvation is written from a series of seven powerful addresses preached at Tylers Green. It is a forthright and experimental exposition of Isaiah 12:3, 'Therefore with joy shall ye draw water out of the wells of salvation.'

John Metcalfe is acknowledged to be perhaps the most gifted expositor and powerful preacher of our day and this is to be seen clearly in The Wells of Salvation.

Price £1.50 *(postage extra)*
(Laminated Cover)
ISBN 0 9502515 6 9

OF GOD OR MAN?

LIGHT FROM GALATIANS

The Epistle to the Galatians contends for deliverance from the law and from carnal ministry.

The Apostle opens his matter in two ways:

Firstly, Paul vindicates himself and his ministry against those that came not from God above, but from Jerusalem below.

Secondly, he defends the Gospel and evangelical liberty against legal perversions and bondage to the flesh.

Price £1.45 *(postage extra)*
(Laminated Cover)
ISBN 0 9506366 3 0

A QUESTION FOR POPE JOHN PAUL II

As a consequence of his many years spent apart in prayer, lonely vigil, and painstaking study of the scripture, John Metcalfe asks a question and looks for an answer from Pope John Paul II.

Price £1.25. *(postage extra)*
(Laminated Cover)
ISBN 0 9506366 4 9

THE BOOK OF RUTH

The Book of Ruth is set against the farming background of old testament Israel at the time of the Judges, the narrative—unfolding the work of God in redemption—being marked by a series of agricultural events.

These events—the famine; the barley harvest; the wheat harvest; the winnowing—possessed a hidden spiritual significance to that community, but, much more, they speak in figure directly to our own times, as the book reveals.

Equally contemporary appear the characters of Ruth, Naomi, Boaz, and the first kinsman, drawn with spiritual perception greatly to the profit of the reader.

Price £4.95 *(postage extra)*
Hardback 200 pages
Laminated bookjacket
Printed, sewn and bound
by the John Metcalfe Publishing Trust
ISBN 1 870039 17 3

PRESENT-DAY CONVERSIONS
OF THE NEW TESTAMENT KIND

FROM THE MINISTRY OF

JOHN METCALFE

The outstandingly striking presentation of this fascinating paperback will surely catch the eye, as its title and contents will certainly captivate the mind: here is a unique publication.

Woven into a gripping narrative, over twenty-one short life stories, all centred on conversions that simply could not have happened had not God broken in, and had not Christ been revealed, the book presents a tremendous challenge, at once moving and thrilling to the reader.

Price £2.25 *(postage extra)*
(Laminated Cover)
Printed, sewn and bound
by the John Metcalfe Publishing Trust
ISBN 1 870039 31 9

DIVINE MEDITATIONS

OF

WILLIAM HUNTINGTON

Originally published by Mr. Huntington as a series of letters to J. Jenkins, under the title of 'Contemplations on the God of Israel', the spiritual content of this correspondence has been skilfully and sympathetically edited, abridged, and arranged so as to form a series of meditations, suitable for daily readings.

Mr. Huntington's own text is thereby adapted to speak directly to the reader in a way much more suited to his ministering immediately to ourselves, in our own circumstances and times.

It is greatly hoped that many today will benefit from this adaption which carefully retains both the spirit and the letter of the text. If any prefer the original format, this is readily available from several sources and many libraries.

Nevertheless, the publishers believe the much more readable form into which Mr. Huntington's very words have been adapted will appeal to a far wider audience, for whose comfort and consolation this carefully edited work has been published.

Price £2.35 (postage extra)
(Laminated Cover)
Printed, sewn and bound
by the John Metcalfe Publishing Trust
ISBN 1 870039 24 6

SAVING FAITH

The sevenfold work of the Holy Ghost in bringing a sinner to saving faith in Christ opened and enlarged.

True faith is the work of God. False faith is the presumption of man. But where is the difference? *Saving Faith* shows the difference.

Price £2.25 *(postage extra)*
Paperback 250 pages
(Laminated Cover)
Printed, sewn and bound
by the John Metcalfe Publishing Trust
ISBN 1 870039 40 8

DELIVERANCE FROM THE LAW
THE WESTMINSTER CONFESSION EXPLODED

Deliverance from the law. A devastating vindication of the gospel of Christ against the traditions of man.

Price £1.90 *(postage extra)*
Paperback 160 pages
(Laminated Cover)
Printed, sewn and bound
by the John Metcalfe Publishing Trust
ISBN 1 870039 41 6

NEWLY PUBLISHED

THE BEATITUDES

A unique insight destined to be the classic opening of this wonderful sequence of utterances from the lips of Jesus.

The reader will discover a penetration of the spiritual heights and divine depths of these peerless words in a way ever fresh and always rewarding though read time and time again.

Price £1.90 *(postage extra)*
Paperback 185 pages
(Laminated cover)
Printed, sewn and bound
by the John Metcalfe Publishing Trust
ISBN 1 870039 45 9

NEWLY PUBLISHED
PHILIPPIANS

The Epistle of Paul the Apostle to the Philippians is opened
by this work from the pen of John Metcalfe with that lucid
thoroughness which one has come to expect from a ministry
received 'not of men, neither by man, but by the revelation of
Jesus Christ'.

The work of God at Philippi is traced 'from the first day' until
the time at which the epistle was written. Never were Lydia
or the Philippian jailor drawn with more lively insight. The
epistle itself is revealed in order, with passages—such as 'the
mind that was in Christ Jesus'—that evidence the work of no
less than a divine for our own times.

The Trustees give glory and thanks to God for the privilege
of producing this book.

Price £1.90 *(postage extra)*
Paperback 185 pages
(Laminated cover)
Printed, sewn and bound
by the John Metcalfe Publishing Trust
ISBN 1 870039 56 4

'TRACT FOR THE TIMES' SERIES

THE GOSPEL OF GOD

'TRACT FOR THE TIMES' SERIES

The Gospel of God. Beautifully designed, this tract positively describes the gospel under the following headings: The Gospel is of God; The Gospel is Entirely of God; The Gospel is Entire in Itself; The Gospel is Preached; The Gospel Imparts Christ; and, Nothing But the Gospel Imparts Christ.

Price 25p *(postage extra)*
(Laminated Cover)
No. 1 in the Series

THE STRAIT GATE

'TRACT FOR THE TIMES' SERIES

The Strait Gate. Exceptionally well made, this booklet consists of extracts from 'The Messiah', compiled in such a way as to challenge the shallowness of much of today's 'easy-believism', whilst positively pointing to the strait gate.

Price 25p *(postage extra)*
(Laminated Cover)
No. 2 in the Series

ETERNAL SONSHIP
AND TAYLOR BRETHREN

'TRACT FOR THE TIMES' SERIES

Eternal Sonship and Taylor Brethren. This booklet is highly recommended, particularly for those perplexed by James Taylor's teaching against the eternal sonship of Christ.

Price 25p *(postage extra)*
(Laminated Cover)
No. 3 in the Series

MARKS OF THE
NEW TESTAMENT CHURCH

'TRACT FOR THE TIMES' SERIES

Marks of the New Testament Church. This exposition from Acts 2:42 declares what were, and what were not, the abiding marks of the church. The apostles' doctrine, fellowship and ordinances are lucidly explained.

Price 25p *(postage extra)*
(Laminated Cover)
No. 4 in the Series

THE CHARISMATIC DELUSION

'TRACT FOR THE TIMES' SERIES

The Charismatic Delusion. A prophetic message revealing the fundamental error of this movement which has swept away so many in the tide of its popularity. Here the delusion is dispelled.

Price 25p *(postage extra)*
(Laminated Cover)
No. 5 in the Series

PREMILLENNIALISM EXPOSED

'TRACT FOR THE TIMES' SERIES

Premillennialism Exposed. Well received evangelically, particularly through the influence of J.N. Darby, the Schofield bible, and the Plymouth Brethren, Premillennialism has assumed the cloak of orthodoxy. In this tract the cloak is removed, and the unorthodoxy of this system is exposed. A remarkable revelation.

Price 25p *(postage extra)*
(Laminated Cover)
No. 6 in the Series

JUSTIFICATION AND PEACE

'TRACT FOR THE TIMES' SERIES

Justification and Peace. This tract is taken from a message preached in December 1984 at Penang Hill, Malaysia. In this well-known address, peace with God is seen to be based upon nothing save justification by faith. No one should miss this tract.

Price 25p *(postage extra)*
(Laminated Cover)
No. 7 in the Series

FAITH OR PRESUMPTION?

'TRACT FOR THE TIMES' SERIES

Faith or presumption? The eighth tract in this vital series exposes the difference between faith and presumption, showing that faith is not of the law, neither is is apart from the work of God, nor is it of man. The work of God in man that precedes saving faith is opened generally and particularly, and the tract goes on to reveal positively the nature of saving faith. Belief and 'easy-believism' are contrasted, making clear the difference between the two, as the system of presumption—called easy-believism—is clearly shown, and the way of true belief pointed out with lucid clarity.

Price 25p *(postage extra)*
(Laminated Cover)
No. 8 in the Series

THE ELECT UNDECEIVED

'TRACT FOR THE TIMES' SERIES

The Elect undeceived, the ninth Tract for the Times, earnestly contends for 'the faith once delivered to the saints' in a way that is spiritually edifying, positive, and subject to the Lord Jesus Christ according to the scriptures.

The Tract is a response to the pamphlet 'Salvation and the Church' published jointly by the Catholic Truth Society and Church House Publishing, in which the Anglican and Roman Catholic Commissioners agree together about JUSTIFICATION. The pamphlet shows how they have agreed.

Price 25p (*postage extra*)
(Laminated Cover)
No. 9 in the Series

JUSTIFYING RIGHTEOUSNESS

'TRACT FOR THE TIMES' SERIES

Justifying Righteousness. Was it wrought by the law of Moses or by the blood of Christ? Written not in the language of dead theology but that of the living God, here is the vital and experimental doctrine of the new testament. Part of the book 'Justification by Faith', nevertheless this tract has a message in itself essential to those who would know and understand the truth.

Price 25p (*postage extra*)
(Laminated Cover)
No. 10 in the Series

RIGHTEOUSNESS IMPUTED

'TRACT FOR THE TIMES' SERIES

Righteousness Imputed. The truth of the gospel and the fallacy of tradition. Here the gospel trumpet of the jubilee is sounded in no uncertain terms, as on the one hand that truth essential to be believed for salvation is opened from holy scripture, and on the other the errors of Brethrenism are brought to light in a unique and enlightening way. This tract is taken from the book 'Justification by Faith', but in itself it conveys a message of great penetration and clarity.

Price 25p *(postage extra)*
(Laminated Cover)
No. 11 in the Series

THE GREAT DECEPTION

'TRACT FOR THE TIMES' SERIES

The Great Deception. The erosion of Justification by faith. All ministers, every Christian, and each assembly ought not only to possess but to read and reread this prophetic message as the word of the Lord to this generation, set in the context of the age. This tract is part of the book 'Justification by Faith' but contains within itself a message which is at once vital and authoritative.

Price 25p *(postage extra)*
(Laminated Cover)
No. 12 in the Series

A FAMINE IN THE LAND

A Famine in the Land. Taken from the Book of Ruth, with telling forcefulness this tract opens conditions exactly parallel to those of our own times. 'Behold, the days come, saith the Lord GOD, that I will send a famine in the land, not a famine of bread, nor a thirst for water, but of hearing the words of the LORD: and they shall wander from sea to sea, and from the north even to the east, they shall run to and fro to seek the word of the LORD, and shall not find it.'

Price 25p *(postage extra)*
(Laminated Cover)
No. 13 in the Series

BLOOD AND WATER

Blood and Water. Of the four gospels, only John reveals the truth that blood was shed at the cross. When it was shed, Jesus was dead already. With the blood there came forth water. But what do these things mean? With devastating present-day application, this tract tells you what they mean.

Price 25p *(postage extra)*
(Laminated Cover)
No. 14 in the Series

WOMEN BISHOPS?
'TRACT FOR THE TIMES' SERIES

Women Bishops? This is a question that has arisen in America, but should it have arisen at all?
Read this tract and find out the authoritative answer.

Price 25p *(postage extra)*
(Laminated Cover)
No. 15 in the Series

THE HEAVENLY VISION
'TRACT FOR THE TIMES' SERIES

The Heavenly Vision not only transformed the prophet himself, it became a savour of life unto life—or death unto death—to all the people.
'*Where there is no vision the people perish*', Proverbs 29:18. This is true. But where is the vision today? And what is the vision today? This tract answers those questions.

Price 25p *(Postage extra)*
(Laminated Cover)
No. 16 in the Series

EVANGELICAL TRACTS

EVANGELICAL TRACTS

1. **The Two Prayers of Elijah.** Green card cover, price 10p.

2. **Wounded for our Transgressions.** Gold card cover, price 10p.

3. **The Blood of Sprinkling.** Red card cover, price 10p.

4. **The Grace of God that brings Salvation.** Blue card cover, price 10p.

5. **The Name of Jesus.** Rose card cover, price 10p.

6. **The Ministry of the New Testament.** Purple card cover, price 10p.

7. **The Death of the Righteous** (*The closing days of J.B. Stoney*) by A.M.S. (his daughter). Ivory card cover, Price 10p.

8. **Repentance.** Sky blue card cover, price 10p.

9. **Legal Deceivers Exposed.** Crimson card cover, price 10p.

10. **Unconditional Salvation.** Green card cover, price 10p.

11. **Religious Merchandise.** Brown card cover, price 10p.

12. **Comfort.** Pink card cover, price 10p.

13. **Peace.** Grey card cover, price 10p.

14. **Eternal Life.** Cobalt card cover, price 10p.

ECCLESIA TRACTS

ECCLESIA TRACTS

The Beginning of the Ecclesia by John Metcalfe. No. 1 in the Series, Sand grain cover, Price 10p.

Churches and the Church by J.N. Darby. Edited. No. 2 in the Series, Sand grain cover, Price 10p.

The Ministers of Christ by John Metcalfe. No. 3 in the Series, Sand grain cover, Price 10p.

The Inward Witness by George Fox. Edited. No. 4 in the Series, Sand grain cover, Price 10p.

The Notion of a Clergyman by J.N. Darby. Edited. No. 5 in the Series, Sand grain cover, Price 10p.

The Servant of the Lord by William Huntington. Edited and Abridged. No. 6 in the Series, Sand grain cover, Price 10p.

One Spirit by William Kelly. Edited. No. 7 in the Series, Sand grain cover, Price 10p.

The Funeral of Arminianism by William Huntington. Edited and Abridged. No. 8 in the Series, Sand grain cover, Price 10p.

One Body by William Kelly. Edited. No. 9 in the Series, Sand grain cover, Price 10p.

False Churches and True by John Metcalfe. No. 10 in the Series, Sand grain cover, Price 10p.

Separation from Evil by J.N. Darby. Edited. No. 11 in the Series, Sand grain cover, Price 10p.

The Remnant by J.B. Stoney. Edited. No. 12 in the Series, Sand grain cover, Price 10p.

The Arminian Skeleton by William Huntington. Edited and Abridged. No. 13 in the Series, Sand grain cover, Price 10p.

FOUNDATION TRACTS

FOUNDATION TRACTS

1. **Female Priests?** by John Metcalfe. Oatmeal cover, price 25p.

2. **The Bondage of the Will** by Martin Luther. Translated and Abridged. Oatmeal cover, price 25p.

3. **Of the Popish Mass** by John Calvin. Translated and Abridged. Oatmeal cover, price 25p.

4. **The Adversary** by John Metcalfe. Oatmeal cover, price 25p.

MINISTRY BY JOHN METCALFE

TAPE MINISTRY BY JOHN METCALFE
FROM ENGLAND AND THE FAR EAST
IS AVAILABLE.

In order to obtain this free recorded ministry, please send your blank cassette (C.90) and the cost of the return postage, including your name and address in block capitals, to the John Metcalfe Publishing Trust, Church Road, Tylers Green, Penn, Bucks, HP10 8LN. Tapelists are available on request.

Owing to the increased demand for the tape ministry, we are unable to supply more than two tapes per order, except in the case of meetings for the hearing of tapes, where a special arrangement can be made.

THE MINISTRY OF THE NEW TESTAMENT

The purpose of this substantial A4 gloss paper magazine is to provide spiritual and experimental ministry with sound doctrine which rightly and prophetically divides the Word of Truth.

Readers of our books will already know the high standards of our publications. They can be confident that these pages will maintain that quality, by giving access to enduring ministry from the past, much of which is derived from sources that are virtually unobtainable today, and publishing a living ministry from the present. Selected articles from the following writers have already been included:

ELI ASHDOWN · ABRAHAM BOOTH · JOHN BRADFORD
JOHN BUNYAN · JOHN BURGON · JOHN CALVIN · DONALD CARGILL
JOHN CENNICK · J.N. DARBY · GEORGE FOX · JOHN FOXE
WILLIAM GADSBY · GREY HAZLERIGG · WILLIAM HUNTINGTON
WILLIAM KELLY · JOHN KENNEDY · JOHN KERSHAW · HANSERD KNOLLYS
JAMES LEWIS · MARTIN LUTHER · ROBERT MURRAY MCCHEYNE
JOHN METCALFE · ALEXANDER—SANDY—PEDEN · J.C. PHILPOT
J.K. POPHAM · JAMES RENWICK · J.B. STONEY · HENRY TANNER
ARTHUR TRIGGS · JOHN VINALL · JOHN WARBURTON
JOHN WELWOOD · GEORGE WHITEFIELD · J.A. WYLIE

Price £1.75 (postage included)
Issued Spring, Summer, Autumn, Winter.

Book Order Form

Please send to the address below:-

	Price	Quantity
A Question for Pope John Paul II	£1.25	......
Of God or Man?	£1.45	......
Noah and the Flood	£1.90	......
Divine Footsteps	£0.95	......
The Red Heifer	£0.75	......
The Wells of Salvation	£1.50	......
The Book of Ruth (Hardback edition)	£4.95	......
Divine Meditations of William Huntington	£2.35	......
Present-Day Conversions of the New Testament Kind	£2.25	......
Saving Faith	£2.25	......
Deliverance from the Law	£1.90	......
The Beatitudes	£1.90	......
Colossians	£0.95	......
Philippians	£1.90	......

Psalms, Hymns & Spiritual Songs (Hardback edition)

	Price	Quantity
The Psalms of the Old Testament	£2.50	......
Spiritual Songs from the Gospels	£2.50	......
The Hymns of the New Testament	£2.50	......

'Apostolic Foundation of the Christian Church' series

		Price	Quantity
Foundations Uncovered	Vol.I	£0.75	......
The Birth of Jesus Christ	Vol.II	£0.95	......
The Messiah (Hardback edition)	Vol.III	£7.75	......
The Son of God and Seed of David (Hardback edition)	Vol.IV	£6.95	......
Christ Crucified (Hardback edition)	Vol.V	£6.95	......
Justification by Faith (Hardback edition)	Vol.VI	£7.50	......
The Church: What is it? (Hardback edition)	Vol.VII	£7.75	......

Name and Address (in block capitals)

. . . .

. . . .

. . . .

If money is sent with order please allow for postage. Please address to:- The John Metcalfe Publishing Trust, Church Road, Tylers Green, Penn, Bucks, HP10 8LN.

Tract Order Form

Please send to the address below:-

		Price	Quantity
Evangelical Tracts			
The Two Prayers of Elijah		£0.10	......
Wounded for our Transgressions		£0.10	......
The Blood of Sprinkling		£0.10	......
The Grace of God that Brings Salvation		£0.10	......
The Name of Jesus		£0.10	......
The Ministry of the New Testament		£0.10	......
The Death of the Righteous by A.M.S.		£0.10	......
Repentance		£0.10	......
Legal Deceivers Exposed		£0.10	......
Unconditional Salvation		£0.10	......
Religious Merchandise		£0.10	......
Comfort		£0.10	......
Peace		£0.10	......
Eternal Life		£0.10	......
'Tract for the Times' series			
The Gospel of God	No.1	£0.25	......
The Strait Gate	No.2	£0.25	......
Eternal Sonship and Taylor Brethren	No.3	£0.25	......
Marks of the New Testament Church	No.4	£0.25	......
The Charismatic Delusion	No.5	£0.25	......
Premillennialism Exposed	No.6	£0.25	......
Justification and Peace	No.7	£0.25	......
Faith or presumption?	No.8	£0.25	......
The Elect undeceived	No.9	£0.25	......
Justifying Righteousness	No.10	£0.25	......
Righteousness Imputed	No.11	£0.25	......
The Great Deception	No.12	£0.25	......
A Famine in the Land	No.13	£0.25	......
Blood and Water	No.14	£0.25	......
Women Bishops?	No.15	£0.25	......
The Heavenly Vision	No.16	£0.25	......

Name and Address (in block capitals)

. . . .

. . . .

. . . .

If money is sent with order please allow for postage. Please address to:- The
John Metcalfe Publishing Trust, Church Road, Tylers Green, Penn, Bucks, HP10 8LN.

Tract Order Form

Please send to the address below:-

		Price	Quantity
Ecclesia Tracts			
The Beginning of the Ecclesia	No.1	£0.10	......
Churches and the Church (J.N.D.)	No.2	£0.10	......
The Ministers of Christ	No.3	£0.10	......
The Inward Witness (G.F.)	No.4	£0.10	......
The Notion of a Clergyman (J.N.D.)	No.5	£0.10	......
The Servant of the Lord (W.H.)	No.6	£0.10	......
One Spirit (W.K.)	No.7	£0.10	......
The Funeral of Arminianism (W.H.)	No.8	£0.10	......
One Body (W.K.)	No.9	£0.10	......
False Churches and True	No.10	£0.10	......
Separation from Evil (J.N.D.)	No.11	£0.10	......
The Remnant (J.B.S.)	No.12	£0.10	......
The Arminian Skeleton (W.H.)	No.13	£0.10	......
Foundation Tracts			
Female Priests?	No.1	£0.25	......
The Bondage of the Will (Martin Luther)	No.2	£0.25	......
Of the Popish Mass (John Calvin)	No.3	£0.25	......
The Adversary	No.4	£0.25	......

Name and Address (in block capitals)

. . . .

. . . .

. . . .

If money is sent with order please allow for postage. Please address to:- The
John Metcalfe Publishing Trust, Church Road, Tylers Green, Penn, Bucks, HP10 8LN.

Magazine Order Form

Name and Address (in block capitals)

. . . .

. . . .

. . . .

Please send me .... current copy/copies of The Ministry of the New Testament.

Please send me .... year/s subscription.

I enclose a cheque/postal order for £ ....

(Price: including postage, U.K. £1.75; Overseas £1.90)
(One year's subscription: Including postage, U.K. £7.00; Overseas £7.60)

Cheques should be made payable to The John Metcalfe Publishing Trust, and for overseas subscribers should be in pounds sterling drawn on a London Bank.

10 or more copies to one address will qualify for a 10% discount

Back numbers from Spring 1986 available.

Please send to The John Metcalfe Publishing Trust, Church Road, Tylers Green, Penn, Bucks, HP10 8LN

All Publications of the Trust are subsidised by the Publishers.